THE AGE OF BEHEMOTHS

A Twentieth Century Fund Paper

THE AGE OF BEHEMOTHS

THE GLOBALIZATION OF MASS MEDIA FIRMS

by Anthony Smith

Priority Press Publications/New York/1991

The Twentieth Century Fund is a research foundation under-
taking timely analyses of economic, political, and social issues.
Not-for-profit and nonpartisan, the Fund was founded in 1919
and endowed by Edward A. Filene.

Library of Congress Cataloging-in-Publication Data

Smith, Anthony. 1938–
  The age of behemoths: the globalization of mass media firms /
by Anthony Smith
    p. cm.

  "A Twentieth Century Fund paper."
  Includes bibliographical references and index.
  1. Mass media—Social aspects—United States. 2. Mass media—
Social aspects. I. Title
HN90.M3S63   1991
302.23′0973—dc20   91-10367
                                                    CIP
  ISBN 0-87078-325-4

Foreword

Although the Twentieth Century Fund has a long history of supporting work on communications and the media, this paper, in a sense, marks the beginning of a new phase in our efforts. Over the next few years, we hope some of our publications will help develop a wider understanding of the changing character of the media business, explore the implications of these trends for the public, and further the debate about the proper role of governments in this area.

Anthony Smith, currently president of Magdalen College at Oxford University, is well suited for the task of sketching an overview of the present movement toward the concentration and globalization of media ownership. In addition, he sorts out some of the answers to the difficult question of where the public interest in this area lies. Smith has written extensively, since 1970, on media affairs in many parts of the world. His published work includes *Goodbye Gutenberg, The Geopolitics of Information,* and *The Shadow in the Cave.*

In this work, he provokes all of us to consider the implications of the sweeping reorganization of world media that is well under way. To some extent, the changes in the media sector are the consequences of even wider developments in economics, technology, and government regulation. In the United States, for example, a decade and a half of deregulation and nonintervention and, more recently, a weakening dollar have combined to produce a media industry in which foreign ownership is increasingly common. In addition, as Ben Bagdikian and others have pointed out, control of media companies of all types is considerably more concentrated than it was as recently as 1980. A similar pattern has emerged in Western Europe and can reasonably be expected to become the world norm.

Smith's paper addresses the strategies and apparent intentions of specific global giants such as Time Warner, News Corporation, Bertelsmann, and Sony. While he indicates some of the research that remains to be done in this area, the Fund is especially pleased that Smith does not shrink from proposing certain forceful recommendations of his own.

In the formulation of public policy, keeping one's balance may always be the most delicate achievement. Nowhere is this harder than in developing public policy for media activity across international boundaries. It is clearly the high wire portion of the larger collection of issues of international commerce and politics facing governments over the next few years. But the degree of difficulty is no excuse for inaction. For changes in ownership and approach are happening apace, heedless of the glacial process of scholarship and multinational negotiations. In this context, the Fund is especially grateful to Anthony Smith for helping to intensify and illuminate the essential public discussion of these issues.

Richard C. Leone, DIRECTOR
The Twentieth Century Fund
March 1991

Acknowledgments

This paper was commissioned by the Twentieth Century Fund in New York and emerges from several conversations with Marcia Bystryn while she was Acting Director and Richard Leone, the new Director of the Fund.

I am most grateful to Keith Negus for his speed and diligence in carrying out a literature search and for helping me to organize my thoughts; to Professor Michael Gurevitch in Maryland and Professor Jeremy Tunstall in London for letting me have access to most illuminating pieces of recent work; and to the staff of the Library of the International Institute of Communications to whom I have long owed a great personal debt.

I am grateful to my assistant Mrs. Judith Godley for helping to prepare the manuscript.

Anthony Smith
Magdalen College
Oxford

★   ★   ★   ★   ★   ★   ★

Table of Contents

★   ★   ★   ★   ★   ★   ★

Foreword by Richard C. Leone................................ *v*

Acknowledgments.................................. *vii*

Introduction 1

The New Global Media Giants..................... 21

The Changing Regulatory Environment............ 41

Where Do We Go from Here?...................... 69

Background Reading............................. 79

Index 81

Introduction

Let us begin by complaining about the difficulty of the task. It is to shed light upon a current process of change, still in its early stages, that is occurring worldwide—with explosive implications for industry and culture. It is also to try to pinpoint the social and moral consequences of this transformation—which has not inaptly acquired the name "globalization"—in societies that are, in any case, hard to compare.

By globalization of mass media firms we mean the concentration into large international companies of previously more locally owned information and entertainment businesses. In one sense, a form of concentration has been under way, at national levels, for a century—especially in the newspaper and magazine industries. Even in the nineteenth century, the number of news agencies around the world began to shrink into a tiny group, dominated by French, German, British, and American firms that divided the world according to the spheres of influence of their respective governments. This process aroused concern that governments were trying to influence the shaping of news values—even deliberately manipulating the information that circulated the globe.

The concern aroused by concentration of the media today is more intractable, but probably similarly irreversible. We are seeing an extension of three familiar processes onto an international plane: chain ownership of newspapers, cross-ownership between media, and acquisition of media by ordinary industrial concerns. This means that even the modest rules and procedures adopted to regulate at the national level cannot any longer easily be applied.

Governments, on the whole, do not like major newspapers passing into foreign hands—even those governments that espouse
the cause of free enterprise. Australia, for example, recently
foiled the attempt of Robert Maxwell to purchase an Australian
paper; but the (originally) Australian Rupert Murdoch now en-
joys unchallenged ownership of newspapers in Britain, the United States, the Far East, and elsewhere.

Today, we are seeing in many countries—including some in
Central Europe—information media that are crucial to political and social life passing into the influence or control of people who are not resident in those societies. We are seeing whole
sections of the entertainment industry—traditionally part of national, city, local, regional, or ethnic life and manners—pass into
the hands of managements whose outlook is exclusively global.

Perhaps this is just one aspect of the gradual ending of the
nationalist phase in world history. Perhaps ownership is irrele-
vant to a company's ability to respond to the cultural needs of
specific audiences. Perhaps the very concern emerges from a
nostalgic, sentimentalized, and patronizing view of popular
culture.

What is particularly fascinating and, to some, very surprising about the present phase of corporate change is that it is
occurring precisely at a moment in technological history when
it has become extremely cheap, and in practical organizational terms easier than for several decades, for new firms to enter
the media market. It costs very little to start a new radio station, for example, and much less than in the 1960s to start a
local television station. Once the necessary license or franchise
is obtained, the raw materials—films and programs—are plen-
tifully available in an international marketplace. Further, publishing was transformed in the 1980s by the arrival of desk-top
computers. Book stores have grown in number throughout the
developed world, so that it should today be much easier for
authors to find their readers and vice versa. The same techniques in computerization and digitization are transforming
video production and sound recording; through cable it is be-

coming annually easier, in theory, to purchase whole television channels offering specialist services, and it is relatively cheap to distribute such material to audiences within a city or a region.

Thus, we ought to be witnessing at the end of the twentieth century a transformation of media industries into hundreds and hundreds of small companies. That, anyway, is what was predicted at the start of the computer revolution. We are supposed to be living at the end of "mass" society. This is the age of media individualism, infinite free choice, consumer sovereignty. Deregulation, espoused by politicians in country after country, should be guaranteeing this great opening of the information and entertainment market.

To some extent, the proliferation is taking place. While new media giants are gobbling up the smaller giants everywhere from Buenos Aires and Hollywood to Paris and Tokyo, armies of small-scale entrepreneurs are also establishing themselves. Still, these are all highly vulnerable, and everywhere the talk is of rationalization and takeover—of new small independents taking over tiny ones or all of them having to take shelter together in the bosom of a Behemoth.

The present development, then, is a dual one. On the one hand, a process of homogenization (of the kind that Hollywood has already made familiar), and on the other, a paradoxical determination by governments to encourage new competitive enterprises. We see the two working simultaneously in the same societies. In France, the talk is not only of media giants Hersant, Maxwell, Berlusconi, but also of the Teletel service that makes vast quantities of information easily available electronically to everyone, of scores of new radio stations, of a whole new generation of viable artisanal filmmakers. But the really powerful outlets for creative work in print and the moving image seem all to be slipping into the capacious hands of a group of giant international companies.

In Britain, Channel Four, for example, conjured three or four hundred small production companies into existence in the 1980s. But by the start of the 1990s, these producers still have only a tiny number of potential patrons and buyers for their wares. The new cable and satellite channels are commissioning very little new work, the BBC has barely started to honor its commitment to buy a quarter of its programs from the independent sector, and Channel Four itself will soon be competing for sales of advertising time and may be drawn into the competition for audiences and cheap production. There thus exists in Britain, as elsewhere, a large number of small media businesses, but their lives have been made no easier as a result of all the deregulatory labor of recent times. The potential buyers of their work have increased, but they are more intensely locked in competition than in the past and have little to spend on experiment and innovation.

Independents do not make cheap programs. Cheap programs are acquired from international salesmen, selling off the rights to old programs that have amortized their costs in their originating societies. Or they are acquired by participating in new international co-productions, turned out and packaged in a dozen languages. The pressure to rationalize the costs of software jeopardizes the quality of television that is internationally available. Of course, there are other pressures playing upon major national networks that force them to produce more expensive and often extremely good programs.

The television world has dissolved from a world of patronage into a series of market places. The American networks are still—despite the growing success of their chief rival, cable— the most lucrative markets into which to sell television material, but they are almost completely locked into a tiny number of competing suppliers. It is almost unheard of for an independent in, say, Kansas City—whatever the skill, however powerful the message—to sell a program to CBS. For an independent in Stockholm, let alone Sri Lanka, to write to NBC is like corresponding with Father Christmas. The major buyers of material are either, as in Western Europe, locked into inexorable and inaccessibly vast state organizations or else they are the hyperactive program schedulers and packagers employed by eight or ten mega-institutions whose main interest lies in increasing audience share. And, in any case, deregulation has now reached the U.S. networks, which are to be allowed again to go directly into production for themselves.

The problems posed by globalization, however, go much deeper than whether professional opportunities are being opened up or closed down. The process raises ethnic and political concerns. The new ubiquity—via satellite and cable—of television channels originating in America, Britain, and France seems inevitably to damage the aspirations of smaller nations and the ethnic audiences within them. True, there remains the opportunity for programs in Welsh or Flemish to appear, and possibly to be translated for wider audiences, but as a higher proportion of the total television available is coming from the dominant television nations, there is a decreasing chance of those Welsh and Flemish programs reaching a majority of the Welsh- or Flemish-speaking people for whom they were intended. It is easier than ever to provide for micro-audiences of many varieties, but those audiences are now subjected to the more powerful materials of larger nations.

Of course, there remains the possibility that entrepreneurs within minority audiences will find ways of making commercial channels work effectively even within the compass of a small ethnic or national community. That was the promise always embedded in the new technology. But, beyond a few vaunted experiments, this promise has yet to be realized. It has been government action, in response to intense political pressure, that has brought Welsh and Breton and Inuit television channels into existence; no one really believes that the market would ever have created them. Politics, not markets, still seem to be the only effective saviours of minority cultures. But there are many technological, regulatory, and industrial changes still to come, their results unforeseeable.

In Western Europe, there has been a decade-long search for a cultural counterpart to the advancing trans-European political movement. A rash of satellite plans was announced—both

public and private—many of them, intentionally or accidental-
ly, "transnational" in character. Now in Europe, that term may
refer to a medium that circulates or transmits across Germany, Austria, and Switzerland, say, intended for the German
speakers in those nations. Or it may, like Tele Luxembourg,
emanate from a small territory in all the major languages of
Europe, intended to compete with the indigenous television
programming of a number of countries.

The European Community began to develop its own cultural
policy in the 1980s and published an important green paper,
"Television Without Frontiers," intended to open up an opportunity for the national programs of the Community to circu-
late throughout the Community. It envisioned "the step-by-step
establishment of a common market for broadcasters and audiences and hence moves to secure the free flow of information,
ideas, opinions and cultural activities within the Community."
The plan was designed to promote a shift toward commercial,
rather than public service, European television.

But it also would mean the creation of a trade barrier to
American entertainment imports—the creation of "quotas" in
the name of national cultural "preservation." To the powerful
lobbyists in the Motion Picture Association of America, the European Community's talk of quotas was a blow to legitimate
commercial interests. To the Europeans, the Motion Picture Association of America just wanted to grab their vast new market, which might cover up Hollywood's uncontrollable cost
spiral, while turning Europe's 350 million viewers into cultural vassals of America.

The ensuing debate has been long and fierce; the outcome is
still uncertain. An official of Irish broadcasting suggested that
a new green paper be commissioned, under the title "Television: Europe-its peoples and their cultures." * That summed up
a widely shared fear that transnationalism in all its forms—

---

* "Programmes, Administration, Law," *EBU Review* 37, no. 1 (January 1986),
p. 22.

even when issuing from the European Community's office in Brussels—is inimical to the whole tradition of nationally based broadcasting to national audiences. The opposition was not national*ist* in character. It was based, as is much of the fear of globalization (private and public), on the belief that the world is in the course of losing the logic of indigenousness and therefore a kind of authenticity; where we hoped that the new media of the postwar era would act as means of reconciliation they were turning into instruments of homogenization; and where we saw technology as part of a long process of modernization it would, in the form in which it actually arrived, deprive us of a home while pretending to give us a larger one.

Of course such thoughts do not produce evidence in audience figures. The reverse is the case. The marketplace gives expression, almost unanswerably, to the needs of consumers. But perhaps we exist also as citizens and hold preferences that our behavior as consumers does not reveal. These find expression at times in the political sphere. The fact that we cheerfully used to buy ozone-unfriendly hairsprays does not mean that we were freely deciding that we wanted a polluted atmosphere. The products available did not allow us to articulate a more collectively beneficial choice.

This conundrum is an old one, and one can duck and weave around it. The point is that the institutional changes accompanying the new media are raising long-term and familiar cultural/political issues; these may be resolved before any real choice is made by people or nations.

What lay, half-forgotten, behind the cultural decision-making were the industrial changes that government decisions, made simultaneously across much of the world, had brought about; the deregulation of the electronics and communications industries. This process acted as a booster fuel to the regrouping and globalization of industries dealing in telecommunications goods and services, in PCs and robotics, in PBXs, audio equipment, television receivers, all of the basic materials of the information industries.

The information revolution of the 1980s was a continuation of the automation revolution that had progressively replaced people with technology in previous decades. In its wake, whole new industries came into existence to supply the new equipment that transformed industrial processes. As automation progressed, it became apparent that there was one sector within industry that remained, as it were, unreconstructed, untouched by the processes of automation; that was the vast information sector.

Information used by industry constitutes a large and increasing proportion of the total value of manufactured goods. It is used and processed not only by the bureaucracy of industry—from accounting and record-keeping to research and advertising, distribution, management, and secretarial services—but by all the outside researchers and consultants, designers and professionals employed by industry. All of these remained stubbornly in the pre-automatic mode.

The computer industry created the tools for a vast transformation of this whole sector and achieved, in respect of the information quotient within the production process, the same kind of economies that automation at the shop-floor level had already achieved. The information revolution is thought of sometimes as a new industrial revolution. In its wake, class, gender, and professional identity, all our ideas and attitudes, have undergone a series of important shifts.

The French call the process "informatisation"—the means by which all of manufacturing, distribution, research, and administration are transformed into computerized, digitized systems. All of the goods involved in this gigantic re-tooling of the swollen information sectors of Western societies share certain characteristics: they require huge investments, item by item, in research and development; the complexity of their ingredient elements (computer chips in particular) grows appreciably year by year; the price of electronic components falls rapidly annually. The result is that the firms engaged in this work are subject to the constant temptation to merge into ever-larger entities. Their markets are always potentially larger if they can achieve the next range of economies of scale, if they can muster larger quantities of research money, if they can benefit from the next level of price reductions. *

Further, the market created by the latest technical innovation is always larger; the capital required to fill the gap always more than for the last development. The establishment of the videodisc is a larger enterprise than the establishment of VHS; HDTV is potentially a bigger project still. A similar pattern applies to the new PBXs, to the satellite industry. And, always, the information content of the finished goods grows greater; each generation of equipment encodes a higher degree of expert knowledge—built into chips and software—than the previous one. It is cheaper to acquire and lock in the software—whether it is entertainment for a new form of videodisc or cable, or chips for a new PC—than to add a new dimension to the hardware. Increasingly, the distinction between the two is eroding.

In the United States, deregulation became almost an article of political faith. The goal of the deregulators was, as a recent study points out, to ensure that prices move toward costs. Because the marginal cost of serving a customer—whether with a chip or a telephone connection—is small or nil, companies charge widely differing prices for identical goods. Intelsat, for example, charges a customer ten times the actual cost of providing a transatlantic connection. The cost of an old television program sold to a television channel, or of a classic orchestral performance transferred to CD, has nothing to do with the cost of supplying the software (which is almost nil), but a great deal to do with the ways in which the item is promoted to movie and CD purchasers.

Changes have swept into all of the information businesses—including the old ones, such as newspapers and magazines. The

---

* For a detailed exposition of this argument, see Michael Palmer and Jeremy Tunstall, *Liberating Communications: Policy-making in France and Britain* (Oxford: Basil Blackwell Ltd., 1990).

goal is control of software with a recognized and economically viable market. Technology is not the important boundary line. So long as there is a market, it does not matter whether a particular form of information is tied to a newspaper or to radio or television or is disseminated by satellite. The computer can always render a suitable cost reduction, make the unviable viable. Right across the industries of information—whether based on text or image, on paper or the cathode-ray tube—contemporary economics have come to prevail, and politicians and regulators see it as their duty to help, through deregulatory measures, to serve the consumer by forcing margins down. Thus, deregulation and computerization have become the parents of globalization.

The result is that all of the companies concerned are driven toward self-protective merger, scale economy, constant reorganization, and a search for the ultimate in rationalized markets. Such has been the central energy of globalization. Few really quarrel with the legal, institutional, and political motivations. No one calculated, however, the moral consequences. It is possible that some will conclude that there aren't any—that information goods are fundamentally the same as others and that we all benefit from the results (whatever they may be) of the enforced efficiencies of deregulation and a more competitive economy.

Globalization is one of those phenomena of the twentieth century in which cultural and political decisions are made in ways that outmaneuver the democratic process. Many ecological issues were identified similarly late in their evolution; media globalization is still early in its history. The energy behind the process emerges from a democratically made decision—that of deregulation (in electronics and communications)—but it is an unforeseen consequence of this policy and it raises a range of questions that are of rather more moment perhaps than the originating intention.

The purpose of what follows is not to establish any final judgment—the processes are too inexorable and still too incomplete for that—but to suggest the issues at work and some of the possible lines of future thought and research.

★ Regulation in a Changing Media Environment ★

The method by which newspapers are manufactured and distributed has always had profound implications for what might be called the moral condition of journalism. Newspapers (and other media, including the twentieth century arrivals of radio, cinema, and television) have always had to balance their commercial and intellectual roles as well as the overlapping and conflicting needs of readers and advertisers, proprietors and editors, sources and governments. The essential requirement of freedom has always been available only on qualified terms, never absolutely; the level of press freedom at any moment is greatly dependent not only upon constitutional and legal arrangements and the state of mind of prevailing governments but also on the way that the medium as an enterprise is being managed. Moreover, freedom from constraint by government is but one of the necessary ingredients of an effective media system: Those responsible for content require an overall environment that encourages the good qualities and discourages the bad.

In the 1950s and 1960s, journalists and academics were concerned with audience effects and agenda-setting, with the training and outlook of journalists and creative workers within the media, and above all with media content. Today, in the era of privatization and the worldwide scramble for the acquisition and control of media industries, there is a heightened interest in the way media enterprises operate, in their growing inter-linkages, and in the commercial judgments that underlie them.

We are all aware that the battles between those great media empires that were formed in the past few decades will be decisive in shaping the general culture of societies. We do not know precisely how. But we sense that we need during the coming years to get to understand more clearly the way in which a new small group of industrial giants, now controlling vast areas of the information and entertainment media, exert their impact on the way national and world culture is evolving. Even more urgently we have to enquire whether individual societies can usefully seek to limit or channel the process of global amalgamations in the interest of maintaining fundamental freedoms.

It was not the printing press in itself that inaugurated the past several centuries of debate and tension over press freedom. Governments (and other institutions) have always seen the media as potentially rival sources of authority. They have concerned themselves with the nature of the material (pamphlets, books, liturgies, newspapers, the novel) that emerged from the press and from other information and entertainment technologies. When a single text was produced, it raised questions about the rights and privileges entailed. Achievement of periodic publication in the early seventeenth century intensified all of the juridical, confessional and political matters at issue. Regular weekly, monthly, and, even more particularly, daily publication created a form of personality within the source itself. Regular anticipated flow of material from the same source more intensely aroused questions of moral and legal rights and obligations.

The regulatory systems developed to govern modern communication devices derive from the bureaucracy for licensing that was created to cope with the newspaper. In the electronic systems that today deliver endlessly updated information, we have the ultimate extension or culmination of periodicity—for in electronic mode the information source is permanently present. We have learned since the arrival of radio and television what had already been suspected in the late nineteenth century: information media shape the realities of a society; they interact with the processes of government and provide the terms of the relationship between governors and governed—even, perhaps especially, in totalitarian societies. Social scientists have worked on a dozen different formulae for describing and evaluating this phenomenon. We now understand rather well how the media amplify, sustain, distort, shape, predetermine, the realities of the world in which we live as citizens. It is the permanence of the presence of the flows of information that turns the media into a determinant of reality. Their role is greater than any truth or falsehood that they offer; it emerges from their inevitability.

Regulatory systems evolved to police, select, control, or otherwise demarcate the boundaries between media; to prevent concentrations of what was deemed to be excessive power; to calculate the consequences of media operations in order to counteract them; to make certain that those in control of specific media command the trust of government; to guarantee forms of economic competition sufficient to prevent the evolution of monopolies. It is this regulatory paraphernalia that has largely drawn the map of the media world that we know today. In the United States, for example, the doctrine of localness governing the franchising of broadcast outlets and the legal limits on the number of local stations in a network, added to the controls on cross-ownership of media and other doctrines governing monopoly, fairness, and business practices, have between them created the American broadcasting system as we know it. It is the changing of the regulatory systems now taking place in many countries and the consequent changes in the institutions and practices to which they give rise (allied to a gigantic transformation in the technologies at work) that are today bringing about a reworking of all the boundaries on the world's media map.

Each technological transformation has been fitted with its own appropriate organizational devices—what one might call its "enterprise formation." The characteristic form of the newspaper of the eighteenth century was a printing house that took in jobbing work and added books and periodical publications as a way to use its capacity to the full (which was determined by the working practices of a highly organized work force divided into minute craft specialties). The newspaper of the nineteenth century required far more working capital to operate, with its growing teams of correspondents attached to the new technologies of the telegraph, and began progressively to detached itself from the general printing business. It became more technology specific. Newspaper owners remained close to the world of political patronage, their independence being secure only when their readership was sufficient to cover their increasing costs. The twentieth century newspaper has required still larger quantities of capital; but it has found itself, through its dependence on advertising, deeply implicated in the general market economy.

Since World War I, the newspaper has ceased to be dependent on the economics of the political world, earning its income from its citizen readers, and becoming more wholeheartedly an instrument of advertising, its revenue deriving decreasingly from the cash directly paid by its readers. The newspaper and the magazine (broadcasting, too, in some societies) quickly became engines of the twentieth century consumer economy, their information fuelling the growth of tastes and fashions, their internal economics greatly influenced by the cycles of trade. "The real problem is that the readers of a newspaper," wrote Walter Lippmann in 1922, commenting on the new tension with which the newspaper editor had to live, "unaccustomed to paying the cost of newsgathering, can be capitalized only by turning them into circulation that can be sold to manufacturers and merchants. And those whom it is most important to capitalize are those who have the most money to spend." *

Since the 1920s, we have seen the growth of group ownership of newspapers, and the reduction of competition among daily newspapers within given markets; some countries—notably Japan and many within Western Europe—have seen intensified competition between national newspapers, with a consequent decline in the importance of city-based papers. Since the early years of the century there have been repeated expressions of fear about the loss of an essential disinterestedness in journalism as a result of the growth of newspaper combines, and there have been many fitful attempts to stop newspaper proprietors from gobbling one another up. But the process has seemed relentless, except where governments have provided financial subsidy and/or vigorous regulation.

---

* Walter Lippmann, *Public Opinion* (New York: Harcourt, Brace & Co., 1922), p. 324.

The new economic system establishing itself in media industries throughout the world emphasizes the ownership of information itself rather than of the mechanically produced forms that information takes. Narrative fiction, for example, plays a part in publishing, in magazines, in cinema and television, and the same work can find a place in all of these media in a world market. Publishers want to be in a position to exploit a work of talent across the whole media landscape; they have come to fear the consequences of being excluded from an audience if they do not have a finger in every kind of media pie. Furthermore, it is becoming easier in technological terms to become involved in a wider range of media. Transnational media empires are thus coming into being to exploit new opportunities and as a protection against possible losses of opportunity. Newspapers, film businesses, radio, television, and publishing are passing into the same institutional hands.

In many of the countries involved such linkages have been thought, in the past, to be a danger to society, and in some cases the law has sought to prevent them. To turn back the present tide altogether would be to stand in the path of the inevitable and commercially necessary. Audiences appear to want the new diversities of information that are the counterpart of the new concentrations in media ownership. A viewer can choose to see a film on video, on cable or satellite, or (later) on conventional television, or he can read the book instead, possibly published by the same company. The new enabling technologies are arriving as a result of other wider changes in telephony, in electronics, in the exploitation of space. National legal systems are helpless to prevent the arrival of alien television channels from unregulated satellites, and in any case markets are no longer containable inside the inherited national forms. It is impossible to regulate the media and information industries in one way and the markets for apples in another.

Behind this new drive to link print and electronic media there lies an important change in thinking about the very nature of communication through wires and through air and space. All broadcasting depends upon the deployment of the natural resource of the electromagnetic spectrum, which, until the recent past, was believed to be by its nature an essentially unsalable commodity—more nebulous than land but equally pertaining to sovereignty, distributable by government patronage alone, not really a commercially manageable resource.

The frequency spectrum has evolved in our political thinking as if it were a constant, unrenewable, and scarce resource. In scientific reality it is none of these, for technology has found seemingly infinite ways to extend the usable areas of the spectrum and to make more and more productive use of it. The scarcity was the result of the regulatory system. Newer techniques for managing the spectrum, both nationally and internationally, in addition to new digitized techniques of the communication media, are making it possible to think of the spectrum today almost as an infinite resource. The market forces operators to make more careful and thrifty use of it and with greater benefit to society (if you accept the diversity of information services and the multiplicity of channels as benefits).

Moreover, the development of telephony through optic and other cables means that a communication may pass through a variety of technologies in the course of the same transaction. A single telephone call can pass via satellite, microwave, optic fiber, coaxial cable; but so may the signal of a radio station or a point-to-point radio message. This phenomenon cancels out, in effect, the validity of boundaries between different kinds of information service—dividing lines that have appeared to exist in nature between mass and private communication, between sound- and vision-based media, between text and video, between emulsion-based images and electronic ones, and even the boundary between book and screen.

This has, in turn, invalidated the constraints that formerly seemed to justify, even necessitate, the old familiar forms of regulation. Now they appear increasingly to be restrictive or counterproductive of cultural and commercial benefit.

A new era of regulation has thus dawned, under the banner of deregulation, which is actually a means for altering the ways in which communication enterprises operate. It is a new kind of regulation—a public policy that drives forward the process of industrial and technical change. But as we have seen, this change is also producing consequences that tend to conflict with other socially desirable objectives—among them the maintenance of diverse sources of ownership in the companies that produce our information and entertainment.

★ The Social Implications of Media Monopoly ★

So great are the institutional and corporate changes that flow from these fundamental shifts in technology, and in its governance, that it is difficult as yet to discern the long-term social implications.

In respect to newspapers, we are used to a system that involves both mutual competition and competition with radio and television. We are used to cinema and television existing in a state of mutual tension, but also in joint competition with video. We think of newspapers, magazines, and book publishing as completely different businesses. We think of the newspaper as a lightly or entirely un-regulated medium, but of television as highly regulated, with obligations in terms of impartiality and balance, with prohibitions on material that might scare or offend—justified in our minds because of the medium's (supposedly) powerful political presence, its highly persuasive nature.

But we are moving into an era in which the distinction between the corporations and institutions that own and manage these different media entities is becoming impossible to draw. The processes of the new technologies and the pressures generated in the new regulatory environment are beginning to suggest to managers of these enterprises that survival and further growth depend upon mergers and alliances across the divides that were so carefully contrived in the past.

That which nations are powerless to prevent does not, of course, automatically become desirable; but it does become necessary to ask again what the former constraints were intended to protect or secure, and to ask whether society might achieve the same objectives by other and less prohibitive means.

It has always been the task of the press and broadcasting to

act as conduits for the flow of information and debate. Democratic societies could not exist in the absence of such a facility. But
the media consist of enterprises that function within a market
economy (within the Western group of countries) and markets
are always prone to the arrival of concentrations of ownership
or control and to the amalgamating of competing forces for
mutual protection. In the new climate, there clearly exist new
advantages and opportunities for companies that combine in
various parts of the information sector.

Moreover, there exists an inevitable tension between the dual
roles of media institutions in the private sector, as instruments
of society and as profit-seeking businesses. Those that operate
in the public sectors of market-oriented societies are also subject to some of the same corporate temptations. In democracies,
citizens should be exposed—not just in theory but in daily
practice—to a multiplicity of information sources. This essential pluralism is jeopardized by the tendency toward amalgamation among previously competing organizations. While the
sheer dynamic of an unconstrained market, it may be argued,
creates new compensating pluralizing chances, it is increasingly
possible for people not to be subject to competing views and out-
looks. In the new culture of diversity, the individual has to
choose his or her sources of influence rather than to chance upon
them willy-nilly. In a one-channel society all of the audience
is obliged—almost—to hear opposing views expressed; in a multichannel society, in which providers of information are not even
obliged to reflect the main debates of the day, it is easy to avoid
the conflict of ideas.

There has been very little research into such intellectual consequences of media monopoly. In a modern society, with many
sources of potential influence playing upon opinion, we do not
yet know whether a decline in competition, say, between
newspapers really makes any difference. In 1989, the Broadcasting Research Unit based in London conducted a survey of
opinions on a range of topics held by readers of the three British national daily newspapers (the *Times*, the *Sun*, and *Today*),

which are all owned by the News Corporation. The opinions of this group of readers were compared with those of readers of other journals. While the three daily titles are designed to appeal to quite different social groups (the *Times* is a "quality" paper, the *Sun* a "popular" paper, and *Today* seeks a middle-income readership), all three have consistently taken a broadly similar editorial line on a number of issues affecting the future of the media.

All these papers have supported the abolition of the license fee on which the BBC has been funded; they have argued that the BBC should be obliged to take advertising; and they have celebrated in banner headlines the launching of the first satellite channels available in Britain. It should be noted that with an adequately funded BBC, a large portion of the British audience might be watching it, rather than Sky TV, the new satellite system that belongs to Rupert Murdoch, chief proprietor of News Corporation. The editor of one of the papers agreed that its intention was "to destabilise the set-up" of British television. And the Broadcasting Research Unit survey indicates that readers of the News Corporation dailies are markedly more likely to be "critical of terrestrial television; to welcome new channels; and to oppose the license fee." * This opinion profile is not consistent with the political leanings or demographic profile of these readers.

The question is, should a media enterprise use the influence of one of its parts (and that inflated by multiple-title ownership) to pursue the interests of another? Readers, it may be argued, know what they are reading and ought to be able to discount legitimately advanced arguments that they suspect of being tendentious. But can they? Do they? The argument that they may make a free choice is, perhaps, no longer sufficient in the era of the information of abundance. A democratic society surely needs all or most of its citizens to have been exposed to contradictory opinions. Is it enough for those differences and con-

---

* "You Can Have Anything They Want," *The Guardian,* June 12, 1989.

tradictions to be merely somewhere available? That is the heart of the problem of "globalization" in so far as it effects the workings of a democratic society.

In the West, where information industries are dominated to a great extent by public-sector bodies, the issue lay concealed or perhaps just ignored. We are now living in what is really the aftermath of mass society; the new media environment is one in which it is decreasingly likely that whole populations will be subject to the same shared flows of information, and can participate in a common pool of knowledge and allusion. But behind the diversities there are new homogeneities in information and entertainment. To see all of the implications, one has to look also at the circumstances that are bringing into existence new media empires and a new generation of media moguls.

The New Global Media Giants

None of the new giant media companies—Murdoch's News Corporation, Time Warner, the Walt Disney Company, Berlusconi, Sony, and Bertelsmann—is fully built. And each of these new global institutions is becoming global in its own unique way, and on the basis of its own particular motivations.

Rupert Murdoch, for example, seems to want to build an empire almost for its own sake, or for the sake of seeing how the pieces of some vast jigsaw can be put together. It is empire-building in its Victorian form, highly political in character—the empire being more important than any of its component parts and each part being a fresh adventure. The Time-Warner linkup is quite different; it is an old-fashioned linking of two conglomerate enterprises for the greater security of both. There is no pursuit of private quest or personal destiny here; it is a piece of gigantic corporate management. The Walt Disney Company is different again. Here is an organization based on creative products of a specialized kind—an organization that has always been international in scope and that can see a range of fresh opportunities. Disney, unlike some of the other growing media companies, wants to stay itself while growing larger; it thus finds it hard to make alliances.

There are many other motivations that animate the new giants. The Italian Berlusconi is new to the media but seems to see Europe as his cause. Sony has concluded that it needs English-language materials in large quantity to maintain its beachhead in the world of hardware; perhaps it is thinking, as Japanese companies do, very clearly and very far ahead, to distant future commercial battles over the control of such media

as high definition television. The German company Bertelsmann is trying to break out of the constraints of a minority language and of a culture in which all media are subject to vigorous
regulation into markets and cultures that offer a freer commercial environment.

All of them are perhaps beginning to discover in corporate
and managerial terms the interlocking nature of the cultural
and the industrial. No company, any more than a person, can
walk out of its environment and behave as if it were suddenly
born again, without nationality, without historical boundaries.
And yet the media environment has lost its national frontiers,
and its inhabitants must learn to live in the world market or
lose their independence. We are looking at new processes of corporate development that have hardly yet begun.

★ The Film Industry ★

An examination of the recent wave of transactions that have
greatly transformed the international film industry reveals that
just seven film libraries and film studios fill the world cinema
market. (There are also, of course, very large industries in many
socialist, formerly socialist, and Third World countries, but their
output, though large in quantity, tends not to signify when compared with the total production and total exports of films made
for audiences in the much richer developed countries.) All of
the seven major film companies are based in the United States,
and they have been accumulating their stores of movies for up
to seventy years.

In the 1980s, these studios discovered that more and more
sales income was available outside the United States—as a
result of the arrival of the electronic and consumer revolution
in country after country. VCRs were everywhere. The U.S.
domestic market remains still the most profitable single market in the world.

The worldwide growth in the demand for entertainment
materials and the prospects for future growth are so great as
to outstrip old constraints and inhibitions and fuel a constant

pressure toward acquisition and consolidation. That is why companies located thousands of miles apart have suddenly discovered the potential benefits of "globalizing," even in industries that have been traditionally bound to a national, local, or ethnic culture. There are now entrepreneurs in five or six countries who wish to enter the U.S. film market. The easiest—and perhaps the only—route to doing so is to acquire one of the existing seven "majors." That is really the constituting principle of "globalization"—the desire to enter an established media market that is wholly clogged by indigenous occupants, one of which is available for merger or acquisition.

In 1980, the U.S. majors earned $2.748 billion in European sales alone; by 1989, European sales had reached $5.033 billion. In the 1980s, foreign earnings were rising to meet and overtake domestic revenues, even with the latter still increasing. Those figures help to explain why, in 1985, Rupert Murdoch's News Corporation was keen to acquire 20th Century Fox for $575 million and why the Qintex Group of Australia paid even more a few years later for United Artists. Meanwhile, the relatively small but then rapidly growing British company, TV South, decided to buy MTM Entertainment—a deal that later turned sour. Giancarlo Parretti of Italy bought a controlling interest in the Cannon Group, having already acquired France's Pathe Cinema company. The objective of all of these transactions was to expand into a business that was undergoing a rapid upward leap in its overall operations around the world, but in which the U.S. market remains the bedrock.

Broadcasting companies need U.S. production companies (preferably with their own libraries) to operate beyond their own narrow national frontiers. Production companies require chains of theaters in other societies to capture the cinema-going audiences of those foreign populations; they also want television and cable stations with operating franchises in those territories. Hardware searches for software, and software, in self-defense, pursues hardware. Suddenly the constraints of national regulation and national cultural habit have disappeared and new opportunities for growth have opened up—with corresponding fears of the consequences of a failure to seize them.

What has begun to intensify and even politicize concern about globalization is the arrival of Japanese companies on American shores. Sony's purchase of CBS Records in 1988 inaugurated a wave of rumors. The Nippon Steel Company had for some time been known to want to diversify into more prosperous areas of enterprise and is already building a theme park with MCA. Sony announced that it was interested in owning a major U.S. production company and talk had it that Sony would eventually bid for MCA. (In summer 1990, it was Matsushita that announced a bid for MCA and secured the prize.) In the late 1980s, the giant Itoh trading company entered the fray by financing a number of large-budget American films. Dentsu, the advertising agency, was also known to be looking for a way into the film business.

★ The Time-Warner Merger ★

The linking of Time and Warner produced the largest single media enterprise known anywhere in the world. The merged company had, in 1989, a total sales figure of $8.7 billion. From the point of view of Time, which had an unhappy experience with cable in the 1970s, the merger could be seen more as an old-style defensive merger than one of the new-industry "synergies." When the merger was announced, stock markets rumored bids for Time from Germany's Bertelsmann and Rupert Murdoch's News Corporation. Time was already a farraginous mixture of businesses, containing among them book publishing (Little Brown) and some cable installations (including the successful HBO). Warner had added the Lorimar company to its already successful film and television interests, but this, too, was more to ward off predators than a deliberate corporate plan.

The Time-Warner marriage provoked widespread fear about the survival of media pluralism in America. Rupert Murdoch, for example, had already acquired *TV Guide* from Walter Annenberg. Would the editors of journals owned by a moving-image entrepreneur feel free to criticize the latter's product? Would journalistic standards collapse? Would television news programs transmitted by one of these companies criticize the movies (and books) produced by the same parent company or deliberately castigate or ignore those produced by rivals?

Prominent critics of media in the United States such as Ben Bagdikian and Joshua Meyrowitz, Todd Gitlin and Nicholas Johnson all warned that such would be the inevitable consequences. "The lords of the global village have their own political agenda," wrote Bagdikian for example. "Together, they exert a homogenizing power over ideas, culture and commerce that affects populations larger than any in history. Neither Caesar, nor Hitler, Franklin Roosevelt nor any Pope, has commanded as much power to shape the information on which so many people depend on which to make decisions about everything from whom to vote for to what to eat." * Although the evidence is only beginning to appear, the dangers are precisely those expressed. What confuses the issue is that a diversity of outlets also arrived in the 1980s. A whole new world of independent companies emerged in many countries; these remain outside the newly homogenizing forces, the new global empires of information.

Both halves of the Time-Warner merger emphasized in March 1989, at the moment of the marriage, that there would be no consolidation; rather there would be expansion. Warner was already supplying 14 percent of the national total of sixty-six hours a week of prime-time network programming; its television distribution arm had fourteen first-run shows on the air; it had forty-four movie packages in the market. Warner is also a main supplier of material to the cable industry, largely through its own film studio (its chief market has been Time's HBO, enjoying an exclusive arrangement under a five-year contract). Both Time and Warner have participated in Turner Broadcasting (7.5 percent between them), and Warner also has

---

* *The Nation*, June 12, 1989, p. 807.

a small share of Viacom International (which Warner held onto
when it sold MTV Network to Viacom). *

The Time-Warner merger encouraged speculation on the next
wave of acquisitions. Paramount had been interested in Time;
its repulse meant that it had cash ready for buying other properties. Shares in Disney and MCA rose in anticipation of a bid,
as did those of Tribune and Viacom, Knight-Ridder and
McGraw-Hill, although their prices dropped later when the various lawsuits and challenges to the Time-Warner merger sub-
sided. It was as if all of the media and information industries
felt themselves automatically linked as potential merger sub-
jects as a result of the Time-Life marriage. They were, in effect,
markings on a map that was in the process of being compre-
hensively redrawn. So were their counterparts around the world.

Most of the potential gain in these and other mergers remains
just that—potential. The new vertically integrated media giants
have not yet demonstrated particular profits from such integration. For example, despite acquisitions throughout the world,
Time and Warner's non-U.S. earnings remain roughly the same.
The president of Bertelsmann Inc., Juergen Kraemer, claims
that cooperation among his half-dozen companies is unusual.
Anecdotal evidence suggests that an "internal" production company operating within one of the newly emerging mega-
corporations has to compete for distribution and production
finance against outside independents, just as it did before.

★ Murdoch's News Corporation ★

In theory, a company with the facilities now available in-house
to the News Corporation ought to be able to discover and nur-
ture an author, represent and publish his or her works, serial-
ize them in newspapers and magazines, turn them into films,
finally use them on television, satellite, cable, and cassette—
perhaps even review them. But, in practice, no such tie-up has
been known to occur.

---

* *Broadcasting*, March 13, 1989.

The benefits tend to be more subtle. Murdoch paid $3 billion for Triangle publications (which includes *TV Guide*), a sum larger than any calculated value of Annenberg's enterprise. But in the context of Murdoch's empire, its potential was much greater, because it gave him access to a vast television audience through a print medium—a great value to a company that, through Fox Broadcasting, is endeavoring to establish a new kind of nationwide network. Eventually, advertising might be sold conjointly on Fox stations and in *TV Guide*. A similar benefit accrued from his purchase of Harper & Row, which provided a potential U.S. outlet for William Collins, a large British publishing house acquired by Murdoch.

Murdoch has in recent years acquired Quad Marketing and Product Movers, both based in New York. Together with Kerry Packer (who in 1986 bought Velassis Inserts) he now controls the freestanding insert business—which slips color advertising coupons and other printed material into publications—in the United States. This joint ownership makes it possible for highly profitable link-ups in newspapers, magazines, television, with a possible simultaneous outlet in *TV Guide*. Such deals tend to eliminate competition and open up specialist lines of business with much higher profit margins than previously available. This helps to explain why higher prices have been paid for some of the acquired properties than analysts believed justifiable at the time.

A list of Murdoch acquisitions in the travel field indicates the tremendous *potential* benefits of "synergy." The News Corporation publishes: *Travel Weekly*; *Official Hotel and Resort Guide*; *Meetings and Conventions*; *Official Meeting Facilities Guide*; *Aviation Daily*; *Aerospace Daily*; *Weekly of Business Aviation*; *Airports*; *Regional Aviation Weekly*; *World Travel Directory*; *Business and Commercial Aviation*; and *World Aviation Directory*. Murdoch has also for some years owned the *Hotel and Travel Index,* a hotel booking and information directory, and has more recently acquired Utell International Ltd., a worldwide computer-based hotel reservation company. Several of his publications are highly valuable databases. He also owns, in partnership with TNT, Ansett Airlines of Australia. His outreach throughout the world of travel is considerable and all possible extensions would appear lucrative. Each fresh acquisition greatly enhances the value of the whole portfolio.

This rationale underlies a large part of News Corporation's phenomenal growth over the past six years—from an asset level of A$2 billion in 1984, to A$8.5 billion in 1986, to A$13.9 billion in 1988. Murdoch, his family, and other friendly owners continue to control half of the stock, and thus can pay relatively low dividends, helping to cover the costs (and interests on borrowings) of new acquisitions. Even a profit drop of 43 percent across the News Corporation portfolio announced in summer 1990 could be absorbed. Downturns in advertising sales, slow growth of Sky satellite dishes, are damaging and cause the slowing down of corporate plans but, when control remains with a small group of individuals, such disappointments do not spell doom—they result in a tightening of the management of the whole enterprise. The News Corporation is built upon a large debt, serviced through cash flow; the sudden diminution of the flow, in 1990, caused Murdoch to engage in a number of selloffs and an expensive restructuring of the debt, but appears not to jeopardize the enterprise, nor to alter long-term company strategy.

★ The Walt Disney Company ★

Every one of the new mega-media corporations of the 1980s has a similar story of growth in the wake of daring management. The Walt Disney Company has emerged from being somewhat dishevelled in the 1970s to being cash-rich and avid for growth in the 1990s, under the leadership of Michael Eisner (ex-Paramount). It moved into homevideo, and sold seven million cassettes of *Cinderella*. Buena Vista, its production and distribution arm, expanded its business rapidly; Touchstone Pictures brought out the money-making *Good Morning Vietnam*, *Three Men and a Baby*, and *Who Framed Roger Rabbit?*—revealing a previously unnoticed international shortage in new feature films that it was able in part to fill. The expansionists have all been pushing at open doors; success has come easily, so long as the acquisitions made are in keeping with the character of the parent company.

The theme park business has proved Disney's fastest growing arm and its missionary base for further penetration of the new European market. Disney's misadventure with Murdoch in 1988 illustrates well its particular corporate style. Both enterprises announced with public glee a mutual venture that would bring Disney's marketing skills to Murdoch and Murdoch's access to satellite channels to Disney. The Astra satellite would offer a Disney channel plus Sky Movies for a combined domestic subscription of $12.50 a month. Within a few months, the arrangement dissolved into law suits, eventually settled out of court.

Disney always has been deeply concerned with its image, particularly because its product has a far greater shelf-life than any other in the movie business since children's films do not lose popularity. It is thus in Disney's interests to control every aspect of the presentation of its products, to ensure effective presentation to generation after generation of children, through medium after medium. Throughout its history, Disney has been known for insisting on controlling the circumstances of an audience's contact with its films and the characters in them. In every country Disney tries to operate as if indigenous to that country. In France, for example, Disney executives insist in checking the television studio hosts who present and interpret its films for French audiences, inspecting the studio set designs, the promotion, and the graphics. The company works with local coproducers throughout Europe, but supervises the whole of the presentation in every case.

Its house policy is thus different for the most part from the other media corporations. Disney treats Europe as a primary, not a secondary, market and produces or reproduces every program specifically for every receiving country. It is an elaborate

operation, appearing in some ways to negate the great economies of scale that the new transnational media markets seem
to offer. But it is paying off in sheer corporate and sales growth.
The Disney style is clearly at variance with that of Murdoch's
enterprises. By the time that the Disney theme park opens in
Paris in 1992, every child in Europe is likely to identify with
Disney characters and not see them as "foreign."

In 1989, after an unhappy period of legal dispute, Disney came
to a rapprochement with News Corporation. Its films will be
seen on Sky. The suits were filed and withdrawn. But the quarrel
reminded both parties that Disney does not like to associate
itself with any enterprise that might be liable to fail. Its promo-
tional strategy depends upon the exclusion of anything that
might hamper or corrode its relationship with children—*all* the
children that exist, now or ever.

★ Berlusconi ★

One (much caricatured) aspect of the present phase of acquisitions and mergers in the media industries is the buccaneer-
ing, self-publicizing proclivity of some of its principals. The
Italians sometimes call it *protagonismo*. And when they do, they
tend to be thinking of Silvio Berlusconi, whose name is indis-
solubly linked with commercial broadcasting throughout Europe. His career illustrates the advantages of being in the van-
guard of new entrepreneurs, with excellent political contacts,
in an expanding field and nation. It also illustrates the disad-
vantages of being in a single industry and nation, with no room
to expand domestically and no encouragement to expand into
other media. *

Berlusconi entered the media industry in the aftermath of
the great free-for-all that broke out in Italy when the Constitutional Court declared the television monopoly (held by RAI, the
three-channel national public service broadcasting institution)
illegal. That was in 1976. Hundreds of stations soon crowded

---

* "The Emperor Comes Home," *Television Business International,* March 1989
(MIP TV Issue), p. 51.

the airways, making the eventual ascent of a monopolist almost inevitable. Someone was needed to rationalize the chaos.

Berlusconi emerged from the world of property and building construction but by the early 1980s had acquired all three of the private national networks that were carved out of the new cacophony of local stations (Canale-5, Italia-1 and Rete-4). To these, he added four specialist channels (Italia-7, Junior TV, Capodistria, and Sport). For a time, Italy's three great publishing houses—Rizzoli, Rusconi, and Mondadori—all owned small networks. But one by one they were beset by the rising cost of program acquisition and by early 1984 the Berlusconi empire had swallowed them. Later in 1984, the Italian courts declared nationwide private television ownership illegal and Berlusconi's networks had to close. Within a week, Premier Craxi intervened, formally reversing the law; Berlusconi's fortunes, in Italy, have been blessed ever since. Six hundred transmitters spread his materials throughout Italy. Berlusconi's Fininvest company collected $8 billion in 1987 and was still on a rising curve.

Berlusconi is not only the biggest producer of television material in Italy (180 hours of television programs a year), but also one of the largest producers of films (70 titles a year, with his own chain of theaters) and the main importer of American films for television. He also has close links with the advertising agencies that have fuelled his acquisitions and profits. He owns the largest one. His three channels now reach roughly the same size audience as RAI's three public-service channels.

In West Germany, Berlusconi's Fininvest company owns 45 percent (with Herbert Kloiber) of Kabel Media in Munich, which reaches two and a half million homes—about an eighth of the West German cable market. His investment should soon be bringing in the equivalent of $20 million a year. Chancellor Kohl has promised him eventual access to Germany's frequencies on the Luxembourg-based Astra satellite.

But changes in Italian law could be to Berlusconi's disadvantage—in fact, they could even put him out of business. The Constitutional Court will pronounce soon on the status of a law stip-

ulating that the Italian Parliament must enact antitrust legislation with all due speed. That same law legalizes private commercial broadcasting, while prohibiting the transmission of live
television nationwide by commercial interests; this has meant
that all of Berlusconi's stations have had to transmit all their
material from cassettes—even though this has meant that copies of the same films are run simultaneously from scores of local stations. The positions being taken by the various political
parties toward this curious rule are largely determined by their
attitudes toward Berlusconi himself (he has close links with the
Italian Socialist party) and the level of their enthusiasm for the
continuation of his television empire.

Political skill and a healthy political address book are a constant invisible ingredient of Berlusconi's successes (lapses in
these areas account for his failures). Take the problem he faced
in being unable, as a commercial broadcaster, to receive live
"feeds" of sport and other programs from the European Broadcasting Union and Intervision (its eastern counterpart). He acquired control of the Italian-language station Capodistria from
Yugoslav public broadcasting, while leaving it technically in
Yugoslav hands. This enabled him to draw on the sports "feeds"
and start up an all-sports channel designed for an all-male
Italian audience. This business already has a market value of
over $1 billion—and it takes the sting out of the Tele-Monte
Carlo challenge, of which the main appeal to the Italian audience has been its access to EBU sports.

Meanwhile RAI is enjoying newly restored morale and is fight-
ing back successfully after some years in the doldrums. Tele-
Monte Carlo, now the property of Brazil's TV Globo, in alliance
with Gianni Agnelli of Fiat (who owns the Rizzoli-*Corriere del-
la Sera* group), is attempting to break into the Italian television market. Its ambition is to become at least the third force
in Italian television. There is a further small player in the market in Odeon TV, which hopes to expand, and there are three
hundred local private rival television stations outside any network. Berlusconi's empire thus requires constant political nur-

ture. Nothing can be taken for granted—even for weeks or months ahead.

Berlusconi also is beset by difficulties outside Italy. In France, Berlusconi now owns 25 percent (the legal limit) of La Cinq, the new French television channel, which has failed to live up to its anticipated profits level. It has lost far more money than Berlusconi even hopes to make in Germany. When the French government insisted that Berlusconi's share of La Cinq be reduced to 25 percent, his response was to team up with the right-wing media magnate Robert Hersant, who also held 25 percent—notwithstanding Berlusconi's impeccably maintained links with the French and Italian socialist parties. For Hersant, Berlusconi offered management expertise; for Berlusconi, Hersant offered fresh political patronage, necessary to acquire further transmitters for La Cinq. At the end of 1989, Berlusconi attempted to oust Hersant from the chairmanship of the channel, using the courts to do so, but the maneuver failed. The channel's fortunes have been less than happy (with losses reaching $200 million) and they remain uncertain, since it has been unable to put up a serious challenge to TF-1, the rival popular channel.

Berlusconi's foray in Spain has turned into a repetition of his French adventure. * He acquired 25 percent of Gestevision-Telecino, with two main local partners (one of them an important Spanish charity for the blind), each with a quarter of the shares. He used one of the two to try to oust the other, while keeping day-to-day control in his own hands.

Berlusconi seems doomed to an endless series of minority shares in new commercial channels—not in the Berlusconi style at all. Certainly this could be his fate in Britain after the passage of Britain's 1990 broadcasting legislation. Such minority shares cannot generate income or inspire political respect on the desired scale.

Unable to expand into the rest of Europe, Berlusconi's Finin-

---

* *Broadcast,* January 26, 1990, p. 8.

vest has nowhere to grow except in Italian media businesses outside television. This perhaps explains why Fininvest has become interested in acquiring Mondadori, a publishing giant. If political pressures in Italy bring about a further opening up of television to rival private commercial interests, it is possible that Fininvest's hold over 50 percent of the audience (level-pegging with RAI) will be watered down—with damaging consequences for advertising revenues.

Fininvest's problems are similar to those of other swashbuckling European entrepreneurs anxious to take a share in the new media bonanza; growth can continue to the point at which political assistance runs out; after that, the entrepreneur is on his own, in a hostile and competitive world. The real mega-media giants are those who manage to operate across a vast land mass, preferably covering two or three continents.

★ Sony ★

One media company that is pursuing a conspicuously global policy—in the sense of deliberately naturalizing itself in foreign lands—is the Sony Corporation of Japan. The approach is similar to that of IBM, which presents itself as a local company in the fourteen countries in which it researches and manufactures. Seventy percent of Sony's sales are outside Japan: its self-vision is of an organization that can function equally well in North America, Asia, and Europe, with Japan as a special profit-center. Its managers are drawn from the countries in which it operates. It even has an American and a West European on its parent board, and some predict that Sony will soon seek separate stock market quotations outside Japan.

Sony has already established four self-sufficient and sovereign companies. * The executives of Sony France report to the European executive committee, chaired by the Swiss Jacob Schmuckli in Cologne. The U.S. companies report to the New Jersey headquarters, where the chairman is the brother of So-

---

* *Business Magazine,* March 1990, pp. 52-60.

ny's founder Akio Morita. Sony's British manufacturing base at Bridgend in Wales, which turns out thousands of television sets a year (of which 88 percent of the parts are locally produced), has twice won a Queen's Award for exports—perhaps the best indication of Sony's effectiveness in what it calls "global localizing." * It is impossible to know, though, where the power really lies—and whether localizing and decentralizing are more than a cosmetic or a policy for good times.

Sony's policy is drawn from past successes and failures. Since the company was founded in the ruins of 1940s Tokyo, it has steadily transformed the leisure habits of the globe with a series of electronic gadgets from television sets and record-players to the latest CD players, camcorders, digital audio tape players, 8mm home movie equipment and a soon-to-be-introduced filmless and tapeless domestic video camera. Other Japanese companies have achieved greater annual sales and profits, but none with the same record for innovation and pioneering. Perhaps Sony's most influential invention has been the Walkman, now with annual global sales of 14 million sets.

But Sony also had a major failure—the Betamax video format, which was overtaken by VHS in the 1970s. Sony lost a considerable investment in what many still consider a superior technology. Its first mistake was not to control a studio or library of material that would be uniquely available on Betamax. Its second mistake was to try to establish Betamax as an industry standard, while insisting that every Betamax set carried the Sony name. JVC went with VHS and let others manufacture its system under license. Gradually, the film companies brought out more and more films on VHS, and Betamax fell into decline. Sony went through a similar experience (with its partner Philips) with the CD format in the early 1980s. Record companies shrank from the new format for fear that their record and cassette sales would be harmed. Sony needed its own major record company to ensure hardware sales.

---

* "Sony Starts to Peddle Dreams," *Financial Times*, September 29, 1989.

So Sony, which had absorbed these two lessons, announced the acquisition of CBS Records, for $2.2 billion, and Columbia Pictures Entertainment, for $3.4 billion. It bought them both, outright. The purpose was twofold: vertical integration and diversification. *

CBS Records is the largest record company in the world; its artists include Michael Jackson and Bruce Springsteen. Columbia owns a library of 2,700 films (including everything from Rambo to Lawrence of Arabia)—the largest backlog of resalable movies in Hollywood. It also owns 23,000 television programs, including the highly lucrative "Wheel of Fortune" and many other game shows and continuing series.

While Sony has been a successful manufacturer and merchant of hardware since its inception, factories in Taiwan and Korea can make cheaper copies and undercut Sony's profits—which have never been as large as those of its rival Matsushita (the parent company of JVC). Sony's movement to software, which, after these two acquisitions, represents a quarter of Sony's total turnover, is thus partly a move into a new business. But the opportunity to promote Sony's hardware is even more important. Sony needs to maintain and enhance sales of its new video version of the Walkman as well as its 8mm system; it is a major presence in the VHS video business. It has 79,000 employees to keep busy, mainly on the manufacturing side. Strategically, therefore, the ability to transfer its huge new library onto 8mm, onto videodisc, tape and eventually HDTV could make its marketing considerably more effective and help lock loyalties into Sony hardware.

But can a hardware company, with decades of experience in selling gadgetry, run a creative concern in another continent and another culture? Sony must be tempted to sacrifice its decentralizing policy and run the film studio and library directly from Japanese headquarters. But to do this would be to fly in the face of declared corporate policy. Sony made sure that CBS

---

* *Broadcasting*, October 2, 1989, p. 37.

Records' key executives remained in office. It also announced its intention to leave Columbia to manage its own affairs under a newly recruited, extremely highly paid and experienced American team. The two acquisitions represent the most daring demarche in twentieth century cultural history.

★ Bertelsmann ★

Until the Time-Life merger, the German magazine giant Bertelsmann was already the biggest integrated media company in the world. Its corporate style is decentralized to the point of self-concealment. Every subsidiary is encouraged to use and keep its own name. Indeed, most of its consumers around the world are probably ignorant of the name of the source of the material they are reading or hearing, from *Stern* magazine to RCA and Ariola Records (bought from General Electric in 1986) to Bantam and Doubleday publishing.

The Bertelsmann company originated with Reinhard Mohn, who spent the war years as a prisoner of war in America and returned to Germany in the 1940s to try to reestablish a century-old inherited firm that had started as a publisher of Bibles in Gütersloh (still the headquarters town). Its present chief executive, Mark Wössner, was groomed by the founder for high office. He soon intends to make an acquisition in the East, which will give Bertelsmann a third continent on which to expand in its various fields of endeavor: music, printing, publishing, records and record clubs, video, a little television, and some radio.

Another unique characteristic of the Bertelsmann corporate style is its pursuit of quality rather than domination. While it predominates in European book clubs and in magazine publishing in a variety of languages, it does not try to "clean up" in any given area. Still, its annual sales now approach $7 billion—only a third of it in Germany. *

The Bertelsmann perspective on the world is to a great extent conditioned, as is naturally that of other media giants, by

---

* "Stern Face of Media's Hidden Star," *Financial Times,* June 8, 1989.

the regulatory environment of its originating society. German regulation is geared to the prevention of monopolies in any field. For example, any company owning more than a fifth of the newspaper circulation in any city or region may not own more than half of a television station; in Hamburg and Berlin, in an effort to hinder the advance of the Springer concern, the authorities have lowered that limit to one quarter. Since it is completely privately owned, and thus immune to hostile takeover, Bertelsmann focuses its attention on the issues of quality of product and continuity of quality in management.

This helps to explain Bertelsmann's reluctance to enter wholeheartedly into highly regulated fields of the media such as broadcasting. Bertelsmann has a share, with the Springer concern, of German satellite television, because it owns a part (39 percent through its subsidiary, Ufa) of RTL-Plus—in order to start a pay-television enterprise in West Germany. * But it has always seemed less than desirable to the Bertelsmann management to enter television more directly. There are public sector channels in the field and these are well entrenched; television is regulated by the highly politicized local Länder administrations, not by the federal government; there is a morass of legal restrictions and the whole thing depends on the scarce resource of frequencies.

The European radio and television market is not like America's, and never will be. It is hard for a European firm to get a useful part of that action, and without a presence in America, participation in television is troublesome and a long-term risk. Publishing and the print media are familiar territories where an entrepreneur can take his own risks.

Bertelsmann's considerable financial capacity has furthered its specialist television interests. RTL-Plus acquired the bulk of the new private terrestrial frequencies in North-Rhine Westphalia, the largest of the Länder. Bertelsmann paid $93 mil-

---

* "Egos and Empires: The Publishers in TV," *Television Business International*, April 1989.

lion to acquire the German rights to Wimbledon and to the country's own television soccer coverage, and this will accelerate the speed at which the new television channel may grow.

Bertelsmann is also making progress in the field of pay-television, but, as with the satellite business, by reason of an alliance with France's Canal-Plus and in competition with an indigenous rival, Leo Kirch, who owns a quarter of the Springer concern and is pushing into pay-television with his Teleclub operation. The Springer/Kirch combination is in partnership with a large group of German local and regional newspapers and is thus emerging as the all-German adversary.

As in other media struggles under way in Europe in this decade, the two German rivals are thus reacting, each in its own way, to the problems posed by the country's indigenous regulatory culture. As in other media struggles under way in Europe in the 1980s and 1990s, the main actors are wrestling with the overflow of historical problems—in the case of Germany with the postwar fear of media monopoly as an aid to political dictatorship. They may speak the language of transnationalism and the new Europeanism, but they are also dealing with the problems of national history. Deregulation often takes forms that reflect the regulatory system it is replacing.

★ ★ ★ ★ ★ ★ ★

The Changing Regulatory Environment

★ ★ ★ ★ ★ ★ ★

The new global media concerns have emerged from different experiences and are growing in different ways. The process of global acquisition is far from complete; we cannot even envisage the new shapes into which the media industries will eventually emerge. It is easy to predict that the world's media are about to fall into the hands of just three or four global companies, like the automobile or airplane industries. At the same time, it is possible to imagine a situation in which many new companies, in both the public and private sectors, have easy access to the market. For every line of speculation, there is some backing—for the changes are technological and ideological, corporate and regulatory.

Some companies are so exasperated by the form and extent of domestic regulation that they attempt to find ways to expand abroad. Others are so inhibited by domestic regulation that they fear expanding abroad—at least within the same field. (This seems to be the case with some American broadcasting companies that have been profoundly conditioned by the complicated rules of broadcast ownership in the United States.) Others—News Corporation is a case in point—seek to expand by manipulating or undermining the domestic regulation of other societies.

Some (Sony, Mitsubishi, perhaps) are growing through vertical integration—hardware buying software, as a tactic within a purely hardware war. Some are selling off non-media interests to concentrate on primary areas of competition. (The British company Reed International has sold off its paper and packaging concern, Associated Newspapers has sold its oil interests,

Robert Maxwell has gone out of engineering.) Others remain mixtures of media and general industries. (Major U.S. television networks, for example, now belong to non-media industries; Fiat controls a group of Italian newspapers, while several other papers are owned by Ferruzzi-Montedison; the *London Observer* owes its continued existence to Lonrho.)

Many media companies acquire bases in other continents to ward off competitors and predators. All of them are aware of the need to have a firm base in three active zones—Asia, Europe, *and* North America—if not immediately then at some future point. All require dynamic, risk-taking management—thus the quixotic, larger-than-life quality of so many of the entrepreneurs engaged in the process. But in the present wave of corporate changes, it is hard to separate acts of "globalization" from acts of more traditional "concentration" or cross-ownership or chain accretion.

One might say that globalization and concentration are different phases of the same process. In past times, there has been a tendency for movement from one to the other. But there are differences in scope, intention, and social implication. In retrospect, we can see that media concentration of the familiar kind consisted of a process of protective or aggressive takeover within a single market or industry—for example, the newspaper industry.

★ Shifting Newspaper Ownership ★

Since the turn of the century, in one country after another, newspaper ownership has drifted into the hands of two or three companies—often to save newspapers in unfavorable market conditions or as a result of a general shift in the pattern and function of the newspaper industry. In Western Europe, where newspapers were initiated as organs of political movements or church or other ideological interests, the loss of a newspaper, and of newspaper competition, signified the collapse of a familiar political culture. The attempt to revive and sustain the competition became an important political cause—most notably in Scandinavia, France, and Italy.

The nineteenth-century city was often able to sustain dozens—even scores—of daily and weekly papers. But as the industry came to depend more and more upon advertising, and as distribution and circulation spread from cities to regions to countries, it became impossible for markets to sustain more than a handful of papers. Many countries granted subsidies to sustain a "party" press; chains of papers grew through merging titles; by the 1950s and 1960s, competition was reduced to the point where, in many societies, the newspaper became a kind of natural monopoly. In those places where competition did exist—for example in the morning or the afternoon market in a given city or region—one or another of the papers (sometimes both) would quickly become economically unhealthy. Where a newspaper had monopoly over a given market, it grew thick and healthy—but often journalistically bland or editorially lazy, sometimes dominated by the advice of professional consultants.

Take, for an extreme example, the case of Vienna. In the 1920s, when the newspaper was the quintessential medium of a boulevard society, Vienna had thirty-six daily newspapers—all profitable, all produced at a high level of journalistic and technical skill. But by the 1940s and 1950s, everything about the newspaper—its content, its social, political, and economic role—had altered. The "real" role of the newspaper, as in most industrial societies, became to provide daily information and entertainment for a consumer world. The phenomenon of newspaper concentration was beginning.

Helsinki provides another example. Helsinki had, by dint of a subsidy system, kept fourteen daily newspapers in existence within its debate-based political world. Still, one newspaper, the *Helsinki Sanomat,* pulled ahead by capturing the basic consumer advertising market. Although some other newspapers survived, they no longer have the "feel" of newspapers; their political and confessional purposes came to dominate.

★ The New Media Owners ★

Global media companies are emerging in response to different forces within national and international economies. These global media companies are also the possessions of different kinds of owners.

In the United States, most of the great media combines are of ancient lineage—that is, they emerge from companies founded in the past century. They are much much bigger than they were even at the end of the war and almost all have acquired interests in broadcasting as well as the press. Most of the very largest companies (perhaps fifteen out of two dozen) are still controlled by members of the founding families; some result from family amalgamations. The Sulzbergers control the New York Times, the Graham family is much in evidence at the Washington Post, Bancroft and Cox are still associated with Dow Jones.

Ted Turner of Turner Broadcasting, on the other hand, now a major force in American television, cable, and satellite, is a force of a new kind. He pushes his wares around the world, somehow free of the restraints that have kept American broadcasting largely within America. Turner has more in common with Hersant, Maxwell, Murdoch, Akio Morita, than he has with the ancient, respected families presiding over so many of the big city newspapers of North America; his outlook is global, theirs is regional and national.

The social ambitions and politics of the new media owners are vast and deeply personal. When asked why they want to own newspapers and networks, their answers usually have more to do with power than money. They are aware that their corporate needs may interfere with the information services they provide, and they often feel unconstrained in this respect. Expansion tends to depend on political favors or, at least, the absence of political obstacles, and this tends to inhibit their editors and managers.

One of the most difficult editorial desks in the world, for example, is that of the editor of the *London Observer*, a two-hundred-year-old Sunday newspaper that has passed into the hands of Roland ("Tiny") Rowland, an industrial magnate with significant interests all over the African continent. Many believe that this editor cannot succeed indefinitely in maintain-

ing the *London Observer*'s traditionally high journalistic standards, especially in the areas of international news and the
coverage of commercial matters in which Rowland is directly
involved. The traditional tensions between publisher/owner and
editor takes new and exasperating forms.

★ The Politics of Privatization ★

All of these new global media companies are operating in an
environment transformed by deregulation. A market formerly
heavily circumscribed has suddenly expanded, though with
large regulatory ditches and hurdles at every turn. A new and
irreversible process has been initiated; hopeful global companies must participate or be rapidly thrown out of the game. With
the opening up of Eastern Europe—and, possibly, in time,
China—the opportunities are there for large, well-managed enterprises with global perspectives and an understanding of the
new economic and political forces. It is not surprising that the
new global entrepreneurs have set about their tasks with the
zeal of prophets of a new revelation. Their gospel is privatization, the open market their paradise, and Brussels their holy
city.

The message is applied with different meanings among different groups of converts. In China, Poland, and the Soviet Union,
it conjures up pictures of a shanty-town marketplace or an out-
of-date nightclub recently released from party control in an East
European capital. In Hungary and Czechoslovakia, it suggests
the acquisition of run-down basic utilities by West German
businessmen. In social democratic countries like France and
Australia, the doctrine is imposed upon a recalcitrant capitalism by socialist governments frightened—by the consequences
of their own previous policies—out of their customary commitment to the state sector. Many of the societies most fervid in
the cult of privatization lost touch with personal capitalism two
generations ago.

In the case of the United Kingdom, there is a political purpose behind the policy of privatization: to create a popular share-

owning democracy in which millions will participate. In the early selling off of public utilities (which included British Telecom), two million people bought shares at very low prices—a third of them reselling as soon as the market established a new and much higher value. The net result has been a growth in the volume held by large institutional shareholders relative to small shareholders.

In both Britain and France, government has also privatized state industries by selling enterprises *in toto* to the highest bidder. France has considered doing this with TF-1, the most popular French national television channel, partly owned by Robert Maxwell, some of whose family members are French nationals.

Alongside the positive drive of privatization—toward an invigorated capitalism—there is a parallel intention to reduce the role of the state. In the United States, voters have elected several administrations with firm intentions to remove the shackles of regulation from American entrepreneurs and thus advance the interests of consumers. One area that has received much attention, for example, are the rules against cross-ownership between print and television; these rules have been systematically relaxed, though not removed. (This subject is discussed further below.)

★ The Four Faces of Privatization ★

Graham Murdock has recently listed what might be called the four faces of privatization, which, between them, constitute this new international engine of economic and social change. *
The first is denationalization—the actual removal from government control and ownership of a whole industry. In his view, this has strengthened the position of already dominant private-sector communications companies, rather than dispersed and decentralized information power. That might be putting it too strongly, since the process has in fact (as in France and Italy)

---

* Graham Murdock, "Concentration and Ownership in the Era of Privatization," in Marjorie Ferguson, ed., *Public Communication: The New Imperatives* (Beverly Hills: Sage Publications, 1990).

also helped some existing companies move into the media field, and helped new companies establish themselves as potentially major forces in the future.

Murdock lists "liberalization," "commercializing the public sector," and "reregulation" as the other three faces or components of the process of privatization. "Liberalization" is introducing a privately run enterprise into a field dominated by public-sector bodies, with the intention of creating a more competitive environment. This device has been employed in Finland, for example, where MTV was introduced to modify the monopoly position of the state broadcasting institution YLE. MTV was provided the right to broadcast during prime time on a network owned and operated by the competing state body, and permitted to sell advertising to raise revenue, leaving YLE exclusive use of the license fee.

In Britain, a similar technique has been used to "break" the monopoly of the BBC, with its two television channels and four national radio networks, at first by establishing a rival national television network, then by adding a collection of commercial radio stations, finally by adding a fourth television channel funded by the commercial contractors of the first commercial channel. The result has been not so much a breaking up of any monopoly as the establishment of a whole series of monopolies (of the license fee revenue, of television advertising, of local radio advertising, and of the special subvention paid by commercial television to fund the operations of Channel Four).

This separation of monopolies has made the television system highly competitive with respect to audiences and programs, but not competitive with respect to revenue. After many years, the advertisers became discontent with dealing with monopoly suppliers of television advertising in regional markets and took part in an ultimately successful campaign to introduce competition in the sale of advertising time. Channel Four will, after 1992, collect its own advertising revenue in a limited competition with the other regional commercial channel, and soon there will be a new Channel Five competing with both.

"Liberalization," therefore, takes various forms and goes

through various stages, each one demonstrating the need for further liberalization. It also often makes all the "liberalized" bodies feel that they really are operating in the public sector and in the public service. So long as a major public-sector body remains in the competition, what occurs is not between equal parties: One of them holds special responsibilities toward "public service," and this either makes the others feel that all special "cultural" needs are catered to or, conversely, that all the competitors have to work toward the same ideals and within the same constraints—especially if their revenue base consists in another specially contrived monopoly.

"Commercialization" is the simultaneous attempt to make public-sector bodies behave "commercially" or to better financial effect. For example, in the United States, PBS is funded so inadequately that it must constantly turn its viewers into contributors and its sponsors into *de facto* advertisers. RAI, in Italy, and ARD and ZDF, in Germany, must sell advertising to supplement the license fee. Today, public broadcasting bodies in many countries are being encouraged—whereas once they were discouraged—to sell sponsorship of programs to commercial companies that want to brighten their public images through connection with a high-quality product.

In Britain, the rules on sponsorship are now being relaxed (for all four existing channels) to encourage introduction of private-sector forms of production funding. The BBC is being urged by government to permit independent program companies to produce a large portion of its programs and to explore ways to use its frequencies to bring in revenue to supplement the license fee, which is to be frozen at present levels. The BBC has already experimented with selling nighttime programs and data through encrypted channels downloaded into the home VCRs of the medical community.

All information media—particularly those based on use of the electromagnetic spectrum—are regulated. The purpose, to borrow a phrase from the U.S. Communications Act, is to serve the "public interest, convenience, necessity." The new deregulation,

Murdock points out, shifts the burden of regulatory purpose from public service to corporate. "Reregulation" is a more accurate term, and it is one being used with increasing frequency.

The history of American television provides a useful example. In the 1940s, the FCC, and the pressure of public and government opinion generally, forced the de-merging of two radio networks, creating America's triple network system. From radio, the system spread, fairly automatically, to television. As television developed, the nature of the networks was determined by a rule establishing that no enterprise could own more than seven AM radio stations, seven FM radio stations, and seven television stations.

The networks thus evolved as organizations possessing many hundreds of freely floating affiliates, permitted to take a "sustaining service" from the host body that, in seven major cities, directly owned and operated a major station. All around the networks and their affiliates there existed a variety of linked and lone stations, making for a plural and highly competitive industry. But despite sporadic efforts, it was impossible for a fourth major network ever to establish itself—apart from the linked stations of PBS, with its minority-interest "prestige" programs.

So long as the three majors occupied between them twenty-one major stations in twenty-one major cities, the competition was all for the audience; no real differentiation between different bands of taste could express itself. * Meanwhile, the networks, though profitable, lived in an atmosphere of considerable constraint. American broadcasting was a controlled institution, absorbing the outlook and purpose of the regulatory body. * * There was no rolling competition among the major actors and no chance, it appeared, for a fourth major to break into the scene.

---

* Roger G. Noll, Merton J. Peck, and John J. McGowan, *Economic Aspects of Television Regulation* (Washington, D.C.: The Brookings Institution, 1973), pp. 58-96.

* * Barry Cole and Mal Oettinger, *Reluctant Regulators: The FCC and the Broadcast Audience* (Reading, Mass.: Addison-Wesley Publishing Co., 1977).

But in the 1980s, the networks' audience started to erode, due to the arrival of video and cable (and some successful programming by a few independent stations). The networks began to feel very insecure, locked into what began to look like a declining sector of the television business. In 1985, the limit of seven AM radio stations, seven FM radio stations, and seven television stations per enterprise was raised to twelve stations in each category—with the proviso that no network could reach, via its owned and operated stations, more than one-quarter of the households in each category. As a result, networks suddenly began to appear worth acquiring. All of them were almost immediately the objects of takeover and merger: The ABC network joined Capital Cities; General Electric bought NBC; Ted Turner tried, and failed, to buy CBS.

A very similar form of deregulation took place in Australian television. The restriction of two stations per owner was lifted, resulting in the emergence of a group of national networks from the major city stations. At the same time, Australian authorities altered the rules governing cross-ownership between newspapers and broadcasting outlets; a single company could no longer control newspapers, radio, and television stations in the same markets. A great buying and selling of newspapers and stations took place, permitting Rupert Murdoch to gain a much greater share of the Australian press than previously. (When he experienced his profits debacle in 1990, he quickly merged four papers into two "twenty-four-hour" papers.) Here again deregulation had become reregulation: A new shape was given to the industries involved, but the new regulatory environment seemed to emerge more from the needs of corporations than of society.

★ Regulations and the Distortion of an Industry ★

Many societies intervene, in a variety of ways, to prevent or delay the process of globalization. Behind these efforts lies a long history of public anxiety and debate about whether and how to use legislation to enhance such cultural and other social ends as pluralism of opinion or the prevention of oligopoly. As one studies the different approaches taken, a fascinating paradox becomes apparent.

European countries, whose radio and television structures emerged directly out of government decisions and operate under tight regulations, are gradually deregulating in ways that are fueling a dynamic process of acquisition and competition. The United States, on the other hand, which has employed federal regulation to rein in what is fundamentally a completely private industry, now has a vast radio and television industry that seems inert in face of new global commercial processes; it is as if the whole machinery has become dependent on the regulatory processes with which it is familiar. No American media company is functioning as a major global predator.

The ultimate purpose of all the regulation is to safeguard freedom of expression itself—though this is variously interpreted. In particular, many countries have introduced regulations intended to prevent cross-ownership between media and to maintain traditional local or regional ownership of information sources.

Any unmonitored or sudden change in the way media are owned in a society opens up the possibility of an uncontrolled or unforeseen shift in social mores. Every unresolved concern about social behavior—from drug taking to bad language, from street violence to illiteracy—is expressed through and visited upon the media. Politicians have tended to see it as part of their role to ensure that the media provide the means to reproduce, restore, or correct a society's values. No aspect of the media could be more crucial to this concern than ownership itself.

It is not surprising, therefore, that even countries such as the United States—which, throughout history, has been vigorously predisposed against government intervention—have long records of legislation designed to prevent oligopoly and to ensure that the media pass only into the hands of trusted individuals and institutions. Above all, such regulations tend to find ways to ensure that ownership remains with people who are citizens of the country concerned and judged to be fit persons.

Many countries have tried to prevent foreign ownership of media. U.S. regulations forbid any foreigner from owning more than one-fifth of the stock in a television station (or a quarter of that of the parent company). It was this restriction that helped persuade Rupert Murdoch to apply for American citizenship. While neither newspaper nor cable ownership is restricted in America, as it is in some other countries, a high value is placed on "local" ownership in the United States. The cachet that surrounds the surviving founding families of city newspapers reflects this attitude. In radio and television, formal licensing of stations is carried out exclusively on a local basis.

In Western Europe, virtually all broadcasting legislation enshrines the intention of ensuring that only "fit" persons control the media. That concern is unlikely to diminish, although it is in evident conflict with the parallel intention of pursuing competitiveness in the radio and television market. In Britain, where a completely new regulatory body has been established in January 1991 (intended to operate with a "lighter touch" than its predecessor), the personal records of all intending major shareholders still will be scrutinized. No major change in share ownership can take place without the agreement of this body, although hostile takeovers will be allowed. In France, the auctioning off of TF-1 indicated a de facto intention to allow all comers in the interests of removing all taint of the old government paternalism from the television system.

In Britain, while television has throughout its history found itself the object of public rows with leading politicians (including prime ministers), it has acquired the habits and psychology of institutional independence—although this has been increasingly strained, especially in the 1980s. British politicians since time immemorial and in all parties—quite unlike the United States—have found it easy to make political capital out of attacks on the press and the media generally. Hardly a month passes but that a minister complains publicly or formally about alleged improprieties committed by British media. (Prime Minister Baldwin, in the 1930s, in a famous phrase, probably composed by his cousin Rudyard Kipling, said that the newspaper owners exercised "power without responsibility, the prerogative of the harlot throughout the ages.") Parliament is the scene of endless attempts, by individual politicians, to force sometimes highly damaging restrictions upon the media (more often upon television).

A completely new institution, the Broadcasting Standards Council, is now attempting to create and enforce a code of agreed practice in regard to such matters as television representation of sexuality. In the Thatcher administration, a new statutory authority was set up to classify all publicly sold videos—including thousands of movies dating back to the 1930s. (Until then, cinema censorship had been a voluntary, industry-based affair, with all municipal authorities empowered to decide whether or not to accept the views of the censoring body.) The printed press has in the meantime set up a new Press Complaints Commission in the effort to forestall the creation of a new government body to supervise its standards of journalism.

Thus while Parliament in Britain has set itself the task of reducing government interference and pursuing a policy of deregulation, it appears simultaneously to be establishing new mechanisms of content control. One of the greatest concerns, therefore, hanging over the new regulatory climate of Britain is that fear of corporate takeover will further undermine the courage of broadcasters who are having to withstand pressure from the government of the day and also to protect their programs from censure by new public bodies concerned with "taste" and "standards." The coup de grace, for many broadcasters, has been a last-minute proposal by the government to introduce a rule making "impartiality" in television programs a statutory requirement rather than a professional and institutional practice.

In the United States, the catalog of media law and regulation since the 1930s represents efforts to maintain pluralism in its various forms. This objective underlay Senator Edward Kennedy's (unsuccessful) attempt in 1988 to alter the rules on cross-ownership in such a way as to prevent Rupert Murdoch from acquiring a television station in Boston: Murdoch already

owned the *Boston Herald*. Kennedy's move failed because it was
ruled to be directed, inequitably, against a single individual
rather than a whole category; the attempt was also clearly
against the contemporary tide of de-restrictiveness.

Print has long been treated as the medium of abundance and
thus as not requiring close regulation outside the normal law.
Until recent times, radio and television have been treated as
scarce national resources, the stewardship of which tends to
justify special prohibitions; equal time and fairness rules evolved
and have been constantly updated and reinterpreted. In the new
environment, however, when broadcast outlets seem to be more
plentiful than print, the emphasis on fairness is disappearing,
and some predict not only the gradual relaxation of content controls in the United States but also their eventual abolition.

★ U.S. Regulation of Media Ownership ★

Ever since the start of broadcasting in the 1920s, the United
States has tried to eschew all unnecessary regulation—at least
in comparison with the societies of Europe. Nonetheless, it has
built up a comprehensive set of controls with respect to media
ownership. These have not prevented would-be global entrepreneurs from entering the American market and staying there—
Murdoch included. But it has tended to inhibit American newspaper and broadcasting entrepreneurs from entering other areas
of the world.

The first group of controls in the United States concerns the
limiting of cross-ownership between media and the limiting of
multiple ownership. These controls stem from the Communications Act of 1934. The act provided the FCC with discretion
to promulgate regulations designed to "promote maximum
diversification of program and service viewpoints and to prevent undue concentration of economic power contrary to the public interest." * The act did not itself expressly inhibit cross- or
multiple ownership with respect to the infant radio medium;

---

* *Report and Order,* Docket No. 14711, 29 Fed. Reg. 7,535 2 R.R.2d 1588, 1591
(1964).

by the 1940s, in fact, a third of all American radio stations were owned by newspapers.

Much of this body of regulation survives into the 1990s. The cross-ownership rules were, in fact, recently invoked against Rupert Murdoch's News America after it acquired Metromedia stations in New York, Chicago, and four other cities, as well as an independent station in Boston. News America was successfully prevailed upon to get rid of both the *Chicago Sun-Times* and the *New York Post*.

The First Amendment underlies FCC adoption of a one-station-per-market system, in an attempt to promote the widest possible dissemination of information from a diversity of sources. In the 1940s, the Supreme Court declared that "access to diverse and antagonistic information sources is essential to the public welfare." (That is not, of course, to say that the spreading of ownership has always resulted in the achievement of that objective.) With the same intention in mind, the FCC prohibited, under its new rules of 1975, the ownership (or control) of a daily newspaper and a radio or television station by the same company in the same community.

When these rules were challenged, the Supreme Court backed the FCC, ruling that "it is unrealistic to expect true diversity from a commonly-owned station-newspaper combination . . . .the divergence of their viewpoints cannot be expected to be the same as if they were antagonistically run." * Later it relented with respect to cable television systems, permitting ownership by radio and television licensees—but still not within the same communities. (Today's deregulatory rule making permits telephone companies, also, to own cable systems, but outside their operating zones.) The national networks, however, are prevented from owning cable stations and, of course, vice versa.

Similar provisions limit multiple ownership of broadcast utilities beyond certain points, although in the more recent arrivals among media—satellites, MMDS (Multichannel Multipoint Distribution Systems), and cable television—multiple ownership

---

* *FCC v. National Citizens Committee for Broadcasting* 985 S.Ct. 2096 (1978).

is permitted. With respect to broadcast outlets, there is a new
limit of twelve stations in any category of media (that is, twelve
AM radio stations, twelve FM radio stations, twelve television
stations). To reinforce this provision, the FCC intends to inhibit
multiple control or ownership in broadcasting that extends to
more than a quarter of the total national audience.

Federal and state antitrust laws also promote competition and
efficiency. They tend to focus on questions of vertical integration—that is, the acquisition by competing companies of technologies, software, or services important to their functioning
but that might better serve consumers if left to compete freely
themselves.

Soon after World War II, for example, the major motion picture companies were obliged to divest themselves of over a thou-
sand movie theaters. Later, a Department of Justice consent
decree prevented television networks from engaging in production or syndication of programs until the year 1990. In the 1960s,
the Justice Department blocked a merger, on antitrust grounds,
between the ABC network and ITT, because ITT was a major
network advertiser. In the interests of antitrust goals, telephone
companies are prohibited from offering content-based services.
On the other hand, the Newspaper Preservation Act of 1970 over-
rode antitrust and monopoly concerns in the interests of helping threatened newspapers remain in business—local monopoly notwithstanding.

Much more than the marketplace, it has been the FCC that
has shaped the American media since the 1920s. It was the FCC
that decided which VHF signals were to be shared out in the
1940s to private and to public (educational) use. It was the FCC
that, in effect, determined that only three networks would
emerge in American television, since no major market contained
more than three in private commercial hands. It was the FCC
that, until recent deregulatory times, effectively prevented
hostile takeovers of television stations, thus freezing station (and
network) ownership between the 1940s and the 1980s.

One can read much of the recent movement of deregulation
as an attempt to push back the influence of the FCC and help

the U.S. industry prepare itself to use the opportunities of global markets.

Some think that, in present conditions, it is antitrust legislation which prevents mergers which would, in fact, assist U.S. firms to compete in the global market. There appears to be a conflict between two economic goals that embody two moral goals. The antitrust argument, which has not been used as frequently during the Reagan/Bush years as previously, has produced a lively controversy in Britain, where critics look at the different ways in which the two societies have chosen to deal with such things as the Murdoch phenomenon.

In Britain, the antimonopoly system was invoked in an effort to prevent certain of Rupert Murdoch's newspaper acquisitions. But in each case brought to its attention, the Monopolies Commission, after investigations, argued that the Murdoch enterprise had not, in fact, acquired a monopoly in any particular sector of the market; thus, although it owns, by some calculations, over 35 percent of the newspaper market, it does not own a dominant position in any of the three classic sectors of the market—the "quality" papers, the "popular" papers, and the "middlebrow" papers. Further, at the moment of referral to the commission, no other company was available or willing to purchase the newspaper in question; the choice was either to have one daily paper less or permit Murdoch to purchase the ailing title.

The breaking up of AT&T and the rethinking of the system of spectrum allocation brought to an end, as it was meant to, a whole era of American thinking about telecommunications. Normal exchange values were introduced to replace a system of quasi-feudal demesnes. One issue greatly debated is whether the body of controls on U.S. domestic media ownership can be appropriately extended into the international media market. Does this collection of inhibitions produce companies that are structurally hampered in their attempt to function within a global information marketplace? Is it arguable that the high level of U.S. broadcasting regulation (relative to other countries with internationally competing companies) encourages new capital, both foreign and domestic, toward the print and thus the less-regulated media?

There are firms, of course, based outside the United States whose long-term strategic corporate objectives include acquiring media enterprises within the United States. U.S. companies have tended not to purchase whole industries or companies outside U.S. borders, concentrating instead on the sale of films, television programs, and other software. That fact (which has not protected the United States from a great deal of international opprobrium) has perhaps been determined in part by the inhibition felt by U.S. firms about acquiring operating systems in unfamiliar legislative terrain.

★ The Benefits of Global Operation ★

Little study has been conducted on the benefits or perceived advantages—the economies of scale, the additional scope—that accrue to global firms as a result of international takeovers. One benefit may be the ability to shift resources of expertise from one part of the media field to a competing activity—marketing skills, perhaps, journalistic talent, or theatrical production ability. Overseas deployment of information and entertainment materials and techniques might enable a company to achieve economies of scale. Most importantly, an international company can use the specialist work forces of other societies, which might make possible reductions in costs or help initiate new ranges of work. Further, the global operator may be able to evade national regulation if it controls whole industries in other societies, and may also be able to shift the central energies of the main company from market to market as political and legal climates alter.

There are also synergies of various kinds that can be achieved by global firms. For example, entrepreneurs often refer to the ability to try out a novel in one country and produce a movie based upon it in another; to release a work successively through the various media of video, cable, television, magazines, paperback, and so on, without the complex scheduling and rights-negotiation problems that would be inevitable and irksome when a diversity of companies is involved.

Perhaps the greatest advantage of all is the ability to deploy highly specialist managerial expertise in the new competitive media climate, for only a tiny group of people have become adept at "turning around" ailing media companies and making the best of their assets. Among the forms of and motives for "vertical" integration, that one is probably key.

Finally, there are the purely emotional factors. The hunt for and acquisition of great companies in overseas territories demands great psychic drive and sheer animal energy; the return for the leading entrepreneurs is the sense of conquest and concomitant satisfactions. For example, a major motive among many of the new media entrepreneurs is the desire to own a large daily newspaper—a desire that often outweighs the cash value. Media ownership offers high status in most societies, often direct political power as well, and the satisfying of needs that are perhaps better explained by a psychologist than by an accountant. Owning a daily newspaper today confers the kind of prestige acquired by Victorian entrepreneurs when they received dukedoms.

★ Encouraging Competition ★

The wave of new regulatory practices with which the FCC experimented in the early 1970s reflected concerns about whether the networks—and television in general—held too much power. Because the three networks held so much power, it was thought that there were too few sources of program making within the American television system.

In 1970, in response to these concerns, the FCC adopted the Prime Time Access Rule, which prevented the networks from placing more than three hours of programs per day in the schedules of their affiliated stations (which dominate the major U.S. audience areas). * This rule was confined to the fifty largest

---

* 47 C.F.R. 8 73.658(k).

television markets. The intention was to encourage a new local industry of program making; instead, it created a new market for syndicated programs as the stations sought new sources
of supply.

At the same time, the FCC adopted a new rule designed to
curb the power of the networks even further—known as the
"financial interest and syndication" rule. * This prevented any
network from acquiring a commercial interest in the domestic
distribution of a program or series that it had not itself produced;
a network could not henceforth sell or distribute programs to
other stations within the United States unless it had made them
itself.

Networks also were prohibited from producing (in-house) more
than five hours a week of prime-time programming and nineteen
hours a week of non-prime-time programming. Further, the FCC
created procedures through which independent production companies were supposed to negotiate with the networks. This was
all meant to help create a fairer marketplace, easier for independent (that is, non-network) producers to enter between 1970 and
1990 (when the financial interest and syndication rule formally expired).

These rules, designed to lessen vertical integration within
American television, were suspected of being ineffective from
the beginning. FCC staff argued later that even in 1970 the networks had not possessed the kind of market power that they
seemed to and that would have justified the rule making. Further, these officials came to believe that the rules themselves
prevented the sharing of the costs of failed programs between
networks and producers, which put at a disadvantage the very
firms that the FCC had been trying to assist. During the 1980s,
the 1970 rules began to be rescinded and, in any case, the climate of competition in the age of the VCR, of Direct Broadcast
Satellite, and of its cable is markedly different from that of the
1970s.

---

* 47 C.F.R. 8 73.658(j)(l) - (3).

Many people still believe that the three major networks distort the market for television programs in the United States and that high-quality programs, in particular, are squeezed out as a result of the powerful bargaining position and restrictive marketing practices of the networks. Since program production for the U.S. domestic market is so hampered by rules, it is thought that the networks are deterred from entering the new burgeoning international market for program material. Non-network firms can compete in the international market more effectively than the networks. Further, foreign firms can enter the United States and acquire facilities that, were it not for the antitrust rules, an American network might acquire. (Sony, for example, acquired Columbia Pictures, which might well have gone to one of the television networks had such an acquisition been legal at the time.)

Other recent acquisitions from abroad of American production companies include the British firm TVS's purchase of MTM and News Corporation's buying of Fox Films. In all three cases, the purchaser has been able to enjoy the benefits of "lock-in"— the potentially lucrative linking of hardware and software. (In the case of the TVS deal, however, MTM proved so unlucrative that the purchasing company was dragged into a serious financial crisis from which, in early 1991, it has still not emerged!) In the case of Sony, which is known to hanker after a major role in HDTV, when the moment arrives, the possession of a Hollywood major will be of very great value. No medium devised since cinema has achieved production quality to rival that of 35mm film—until, that is, the advent of HDTV. If Sony succeeds in imposing its format on this new system, it will need easy access to large quantities of films.

In Europe, apart from in the United Kingdom, the hostile takeover is very rare. Consequently, European companies look to the United States—and also the United Kingdom—for growth through acquisition. In the United States, some major—hostile and benign—domestic purchases have taken place in the media field (notably General Electric's buyout of RCA, and thus of NBC), but the bonanzas arising from "lock-in" in its purest form are reserved, by reason of American domestic legislation, to foreign companies.

The cable industry in the United States, which is regulated at the state level rather than by the FCC, largely escaped the 1970s bout of rule making. Cable companies can acquire or join other cable companies, and concentrated ownership and vertical integration can occur freely. There are large areas of the United States where cable controls significant portions of the total information industry.

The Cable Television Consumer Protection Act of 1989 * was introduced to limit the vertical growth of cable companies. It stops companies from discriminating in terms and conditions with respect to the sale of programs to competing cable systems; it imposes the obligation on cable to carry certain signals deemed to be socially desirable in order to earn the benefits of copyright legislation; it prohibits concentrations in ownership of cable above 15 percent of total national subscribers. It may take until the cable networks are fully developed before it is known whether this form of legislation leads to the intended combination of diversity and quality.

Because of the advent of cable, the FCC is having to relive and rethink all the stages through which it passed with radio and television. It is attempting to divorce, to some extent, production and distribution in order to encourage a healthy, competitive market in programs and channels. In an earlier study of the problem, the National Telecommunications and Information Administration concluded that joint ownership of program services and cable systems was beneficial to consumers. The future lines of rule making, however, are by no means clear. What is apparent is that the new preoccupation with the international marketplace is likely to produce the decisive arguments.

Non-Americans may not (under Section 310[b] of the Communications Act) acquire broadcast licenses nor be directors of com-

---

* 1880, 101st Cong., 2d sess. (1989).

panies that do—although they or their companies may own up to 20 percent of the stock in given licensees. This rule does not apply to cable, theaters, or print-based media that have not been subject historically to a licensing system. This is in contrast with the laws of other countries, which do, in some cases, permit American firms to own new and old media outlets. Moreover, U.S. companies operating abroad may benefit from the capital available to them. It is therefore questionable whether the controls on foreign ownership designed to maintain a free and indigenously controlled media in the United States are any longer serving their purpose.

★ West European Media Regulations ★

Every society in Western Europe (and now some even in Central Europe), which has been swept into the deregulatory phase, contains people concerned about the survival of media that foster diversity of opinion. There is no country that does not fear the emergence of a very small number of large media-holding groups—even though each of them wishes to encourage the private sector to be active in the information field. Throughout the 1970s, efforts were made, largely through government subsidy and the imposition of a number of redistributive para-fiscal devices, to maintain a range of (often party-based) newspapers and magazines. * For Americans, there is a paradox in the fact that most of these democratic societies look to state subsidy, and often to state ownership, of media to guarantee political pluralism. But outside North America, the private sector has been viewed with a certain distrust, especially in the areas of radio and television, insofar as the society concerned is searching for a firm basis for intellectual and political diversity.

Today, many West European countries are trying to prevent concentration of ownership in the newly burgeoning private-sector media. Often, these efforts come simply through the

---

* For a list of these, see Anthony Smith, *Subsidies and the Press in Europe* (London: Policy Studies Institute, June 1977).

prevailing antitrust legislation and regulation. The Nether-
lands, Austria, and Portugal, for example, are making use of
their antimonopoly laws. So are Sweden, Denmark, and Finland; Finland also has imposed new controls on radio ownership. The Italian parliament is considering strengthening
legislation on competition, which would apply to the media
industries.

Several of the larger West European countries—France, Britain, Germany—have introduced major pieces of new legislation
within the past ten years to deal with the growth of media oligopolies. In each instance, the legislation represents the latest
step in a constant effort to hold back tendencies toward cross-
ownership and media concentration. The rules are built into
the very licenses that enable the broadcasters (cable as well as
radio and television) to function.

In Germany, a single company or organization can receive only
one license—whether for a national or regional broadcasting
service. There are areas of the country in which it is possible
to receive fewer than three of the new private television services (in addition to the three public services), and here the law
insists that the channel providers create their own method for
supporting diversity of opinion.

In France, new legislation also limits the number of licenses
that may be held by any single operator, whether in the same
or different services. A single individual may not hold more than
25 percent of shares or voting rights in a terrestrial television
channel covering the whole nation, more than 50 percent of
those in a regional station, or 50 percent of a satellite
franchise. *

In the United Kingdom, new legislation has created a wholly new regulatory system, the full impact of which on the structures of ownership will not be known for several years. A new
body, the Independent Television Commission, with parallel ar-

---

* Freedom of Communication Act of September 30, 1986, as amended by an
act of January 17, 1989.

rangements for radio and cable, replaces the old Independent Broadcasting Authority, and is designed to encourage a more commercially competitive environment. But the new legislation allows for (hostile) takeovers of radio and television franchises (two years or more after the granting of a franchise), which has raised concerns about long-term diversity of ownership in commercial radio and television.

The new system does prohibit private-sector cross-ownership of media within any franchise area. The prospectus of every applicant for the auction of franchises (which is a new method for awarding such contracts in the United Kingdom) is to be scrutinized by the Independent Television Commission in terms of ownership and management as well as program quality. Only those that pass the "quality threshold" may compete in the auction, though considerations such as the general record and suitability of the applicants and the likely quality of their future programs may be taken into account. Companies that succeed at the auction (and therefore presumably promise to spend a large portion of their advertising income on program making) are protected for two years against sudden takeover by predators.

The cable legislation of 1984 forbade any cable franchise being awarded to anyone operating a radio or television service in the same area. Commercial radio in Britain has always permitted small amounts (up to 20 percent) of shares in local stations to be held by newspapers. At first, when local commercial radio was introduced, this was encouraged as a way to compensate local newspapers for advertising losses; in the new legislation the control remains in place, but now rather as a safeguard against encroachment on radio by the press.

With respect to newspapers, Britain has always looked to its antimonopoly laws for protection against undue concentration: The Office of Fair Trading is empowered to examine any action that restricts or prevents competition, and it may, if it feels that the hindrance has not been removed, refer a problem to the Monopolies and Mergers Commission. In stark contrast to the electronic media, newspaper mergers tend to take place when a given title is in danger of extinction and the public authority must choose, in effect, between permitting a merger or multiple ownership and allowing a newspaper to go out of existence. To date, the system has not in any instance succeeded in preventing a single newspaper takeover.

All of these systems of control share an objective: to prevent the media in a given geographical area from slipping into the control of the same person or group. Italy's experience with total deregulation in the 1970s has helped to inhibit any other European nation from taking a comparable step. The results were both a collapse in the quality of television available to the average Italian and the arrival of powerful oligopolies in the media field avid for further acquisitions. One of the groups—that of Berlusconi—that established itself in Italy now functions as a continental predator. The present revisions of monopoly legislation and the new controls on cross-media ownership are intended partly as a response to the new threats of foreign control. This suggests a further round of rule making in the 1990s.

With certain exceptions, such as Ireland (and a number of continental frontier areas), European countries have not had to construct national policies to deal with the problem of distant or invading signals. Although, between the 1930s and 1950s, Radio Luxembourg pumped advertising and entertainment material into tens of millions of homes, it ceased to be a real threat to national and regional broadcasting after the consumer boom of the 1960s, when most countries introduced their own local commercial radio and Radio Luxembourg faded as a serious competitor to domestic commercial radio. Today, the greatest threat to the audience levels of indigenous broadcasting comes from unregulated satellite-television operators based outside the receiving countries, and outside the remit of their regulation.

Although satellite operations are expensive to initiate and to promote, they represent a major new challenge for established regulatory frameworks and for national control of the dominant cultural experience. It is too early to tell whether countries will make efforts to keep a relatively small number of national channels well enough funded to provide plenty of home-produced programs (probably the British reaction) or whether they will prefer instead to inhibit outside entrepreneurs by maintaining pressure against international satellite operators acquiring large interests in newspapers and other media.

In Western Europe, satellites present the clearest threat to national governments' ability to supervise the main apparatus of popular culture: television. In the changing countries of Central Europe, however, satellites seem to offer the most rapid path to the yearned-for new pluralism—for the satellite brings the domestic channels of Britain, France, Germany, and Scandinavia, which have traditionally offered the political and intellectual debate that the old regimes denied. Satellite also brings the new information channels of Sky and CNN.

The countries of the European Community are having to come to terms with both a wished-for internal channel competition and an undesired and relatively unpoliced external pluralism via satellite. For the moment, all of the countries of Europe are trying to hold onto at least one or two locally regulated, nationally funded, indigenously sustained television channels—while all around the audience is being captured by new and enticing nonterrestrial foreign messages. More and more it is clear that the real television market is international: The question is only to what extent the content is European and to what extent American.

★ ★ ★ ★ ★ ★ ★

Where Do We Go from Here?

★ ★ ★ ★ ★ ★ ★

★ The Moral Issues ★

With attention focused on technological changes and corporate growth, we fail to notice that fundamental assumptions are being challenged.

Every piece of broadcasting regulation between 1910 and 1980, for example, invoked the shortage of frequencies to justify interventionism. Today, no such shortage exists, or, at least, no shortage in relation to the number of viable print outlets in the same market. Cable, satellite, and terrestrial channels are all increasing in number and availability; every society can fix its own rules as to who should own what and under what rules, payments, and leases. The question, therefore, is whether it remains logical to impose, for example, balance and objectivity rules when the case for these was based entirely on a spectrum scarcity that no longer prevails.

The purposes of intervention need to be reexamined, as well as the morality of it. Clearly, there are problems of professional practice and malpractice, justice, and public administration in the new global media that must be dealt with outside the corporate and professional environment—via public debate. Complaints about journalistic malpractice, intrusions into privacy in the course of investigations, representations of exploitative violence, and the ways in which journalism acts as an aid to terrorism demand public attention.

While concern about this phenomenon has been raised with regard to video and television, it is hardly debated at all in terms of the press—where, arguably, in some countries, the offenses are more serious. Politicians would counter with two arguments

—that the visual medium, because it is more powerful, ampli-
fies the misdemeanor, and that broadcasting (in regulatory
terms) is within the province of the state, while the press is not.
But in most developed countries, no single television channel
commands the attention of a majority of the population, while
newspapers frequently enjoy a (local) monopoly status.

Public opinion is shifting toward intervention and regulat-
ing the media in these areas. It would be illogical and self-
contradictory for such intervention to concentrate on offenses
in one of the information industries and not in another—
particularly when, certainly in terms of ownership, the distinction is rapidly disappearing. Journalists and writers, directors
and producers, move about from film to television, from radio
newsroom to newspaper, and so on, often within the same firm.
It is no longer appropriate for different professional codes to apply to different communication techniques when journalists
work in all of them and when a single proprietor may own all
of them.

Obviously every society requires some form of protection
against libel, misrepresentation, and intrusion that ordinary
civil law does not encompass. And so a single, comprehensive
structure of media regulation and a single structure of public
accountability (news councils, press councils, ombudsmen, etc.)
need to be devised, perhaps starting with the amalgamation
of the bodies already in place.

We now live in a society in which the information industries
have become basic to the economy rather than peripheral, and
it is almost universally accepted that some restriction on mul-
timedia ownership and on excessive information power generally is justified. It is inconceivable that countries that have
taken pains to build open democratic systems will allow them
to be casually undermined by the growth of preventable concentrations of media ownership.

Even at the level of pure economics, it is damaging for media
that provide the information on which consumer choices are
made to pass into the hands of the people who control the in-

dustries about which that information is disseminated. Television and the press are basic sources of popular commercial knowledge; they are the means by which goods are promoted and advertised and through which the underlying need for those services and goods is discussed and the audience/market educated into their use.

The public interest, hard always to define, must lie in the provision of a diversity of information from a diversity of sources— and therefore in the limiting of concentration of ownership. Otherwise, the democratic process itself is placed in thrall to a company or individual that may be pursuing, albeit quite legitimately, ends that are at variance with other objectives of a society. Nonetheless, concentration is being driven forward by regulatory and technological forces. But while a danger may exist, it cannot be assumed that every example of transnational ownership is an infringement of a society's rights. Also, it is important to maintain ease of entry for new voices.

The public interest in broadcast media has always enjoyed a "collective" dimension, for the spectrum has, until the present day, been treated as a special form of public property—perhaps the last remnant of the kinds of ownership that existed in common land surrounding feudal villages or in commercial rights and monopolies that flourished prior to the industrial revolution. In the 1970s, some foresaw the coming exponential growth in the demand for spectrum use, and it gradually became clear that all those institutions whose customs and working practices had been based upon the inherited view of the spectrum were in for a major shake-up. That shake-up arrived everywhere in the 1980s.

In the United States, the shake-up had become inevitable twenty years earlier, when the FCC obliged the Bell company to allow its customers to attach their own gadgets to its telephone lines. At that time, long-distance and short-distance toll rates for telephone calls were differentiated and separated—in the interests of the consumer. In many countries, postal services and telecommunications services were separated into different institutions. The familiar PTTs died. Eventually, though, telecommunications administrations began to make firm analogy between their new attitude to the telephone line and a possible new attitude to the spectrum itself. Large-scale customers were permitted to sell or sublease excess channel capacity in microwave links, and what was once a kind of sacral national resource began to turn into a salable entity. Competing carriers arrived to supply long-distance telephone services. More and different kinds of use were permitted for the same areas of the spectrum. Then the Bell company was broken up. By this time, a dozen new services—from the cable to the portable telephone—had become familiar additions to our lives.

In Britain, in the Thatcher era, officials actually started to think about auctioning parts of the spectrum. A similar move already had been taken with respect to some of the more recondite frequencies in America. It became clear that alongside the transformation in the means of carrying messages, a tremendous change was under way in our conceptions of popular culture.

The proliferation of telecommunications services ran parallel with the ending of the sense of "mass" in many forms of popular culture—the broadcast ones in particular. Video had arrived in most homes. We had begun to think of moving-image fiction as something chosen and purchased from a kind of library—no longer as a service delivered from a distant public authority. The sheer quantity of signals available meant that we no longer thought of ourselves as sharing, through television, a single pool of common cultural experiences.

It was recognized that every society held thousands of small groups, not the undifferentiated mass audience of the past. Information and entertainment would henceforth be based on the culture of infinite choice.

We have not yet completed the journey. We have not even understood fully the nature of the change through which we are passing. For many, the trip has not even begun. But we are constructing the means for getting there. And the vehicle is rolling.

★ Future Lines of Research ★

"Global Media Lords Threaten Freedom of Information"—that is the first of the top ten unreported issues listed by Project Censored, a media research project in its fourteenth year at Sonoma State University, California. * The researchers argue that five corporations now "dominate the fight for millions of minds" and may, in a decade, come to control most of the world's media. While such predictions are apt to drift off course, the growth of global media companies should indeed be treated as a potential threat to freedom of expression. The fact that it has become much more difficult to manipulate or impede the process of international amalgamation should not blind us to the overall *potential* danger.

If the majority of our information and entertainment passes into the control of half a dozen companies (which, in effect, means half a dozen individuals), then this constitutes a danger— whatever the policies and attitudes of the corporate managers themselves. In such circumstances—in the imminence of such circumstances—government itself would come to be conducted at the behest of this self-selected group. It is an unwelcome paradox for some to have to consider whether regulation under the aegis of national governments does not sometimes lead to greater pluralism than unregulated competition between companies in a fight to the death.

The goal of diversity must be contrived in different ways in different circumstances; there is little dogmatic certainty about how to achieve it and keep it. The first requirement is a clear and disinterested monitoring process—a collecting of global information about the growth of global companies within the media (including entertainment) industries. This will help us to chart the course and see whether it is leading toward the feared quintopoly. But it is not enough to watch the growth of the giant corporations; it is equally important to see whether small media companies are continuing to spring up and develop from

---

* See *Index on Censorship,* vol. 19, no. 7, London, August 1990.

other non-media companies. Are newspapers continuing to grow in number? Are the new radio and television outlets passing into the same hands or into the hands of the newer companies? Are the latter surviving?

The second requirement is for a flow of real case history from every part of the world. It is one thing to measure freedom of expression through oppression. We (probably) know from human rights organizations how many journalists, writers, and filmmakers around the world are in prison, and what fresh pieces of repressive legislation have been passed. But that does not tell us really about the moral condition of the media in what might be referred to as the *normal* circumstances in the majority of countries.

We need to know, for example, whether each society has a viable film and television industry of its own, with adequately trained directors reflecting, among other matters, on that society's problems. We need to know whether the government permits an unimpeded outflow of information, whether the education system helps each generation to understand and decode the information it receives from the media industries. We need to know whether the major newspapers are deliberately ignoring or underreporting crucial national issues, or whether they are subject to nepotistic or corrupt control. We should know whether there are problems of access to the media—whether the inhabitants are permitted by law or available capital to contribute to newspapers, radio, and television or to enter the media marketplace. This case history, region by region, will allow for greater understanding of the implications of the shifts in corporate control. It is not enough to know whether a country is suffering from "censorship" or from incipient monopoly.

The new media empires are strange terrains. Little is known about how they operate *intellectually*. Who tells whom to do what within these empires, and by what means? Few are naive enough to think that a newspaper editor works entirely according to his own opinions and beliefs. But there is very little written that explains how pressures are exerted through a vast chain of newspapers and other media possibly stretching across several continents. How are Rupert Murdoch's editors presented with the line they apparently follow? In what ways does Robert Maxwell's ownership of Macmillan Inc. influence the choice of books commissioned? How do the professionals within a company with equally important interests in three continents absorb a corporate view in politics and public affairs?

There is an enormous range of study of the inside worlds of the newly emerging cross-media mega-corporations to be carried out before we begin to get an informed notion of what is really changing within our environment of information.

The parallel requirement, of course, is to learn about how public opinion evolves in the new environment. At what point do readers become aware that they are being sold a line in the channels and papers owned by a single individual? The reference above to research on the views of readers of three of Murdoch's papers in Britain offers but a hint of some of the work that might be undertaken on the manipulation of opinion transnationally in the media owned by transnational corporations.

One great difficulty about this new phase of media research and media mapping is that it requires critical scrutiny of societies that are used to doing the observing. Researchers tend to be concentrated in certain countries of the developed world and are not, on the whole, geared to asking these questions of their own societies. Moreover, the questions that need asking do not lead to obvious answers, still less to obvious "solutions."

There are only fifteen—out of 1,500—towns in America with competing daily papers. This may well have deprived a vast number of Americans of access to crusading journalism within their communities; but has it? The shrinking of the American press into a series of city monopolies probably did not in itself cripple the free flow of ideas and information in the United States—although many people thought it would.

Does Sony's control of a Hollywood major necessarily mean that one section of America's movies will be any less "American" in approach or less numerous—or simply more international and less relevant to American society? It would be valuable to study the impact of Japanese ownership over the long term on Columbia Pictures—from inside.

What we need to understand are the cultural implications of the rapidly changing media map of the world. We obviously bring old questions to the table, but we may well emerge with new questions, with new fears replacing old ones.

Research also should be conducted on the legislative or administrative changes designed to regain or maintain media pluralism, which are under way in various countries. Many countries are deliberately working to prevent cross-ownership and conglomerate ownership, although new technologies of satellite, cable, and video may undermine such efforts. The pioneering work of the 1960s and 1970s in subsidy systems, intervention systems, systems of accountability through ombudsmen and press councils should not be allowed to fade away. At this moment, in some countries, the regulatory effort is being intensified. It is important to keep such moves under scrutiny, because they could provide evidence for those societies currently taking a different, less interventionist, view of how to influence major corporations in the era of deregulation.

Every country is entering the new era with a complex regulatory system in place, but also with the sense that the whole operation is being rendered nugatory. In matters of content regulation, it is becoming ever harder to police the standards that are laid down, whether they deal with protection of children, advertising practices, or representation of sexuality and violence— even more if they are intended to promote diversity. But that does not make the controls any less desirable. The more profuse the flow of the media, the more concerned are large sections of the public about the control of content—particularly with respect to children. Deregulation does not put a stop to the social politics of media control.

A new area of comparative study is being defined—suitable for single-issue campaigns and pressure groups—with the experience of new professional media organizations added to that of old and new regulatory bodies. Plenty of research "clearing houses" exist in a dozen countries, and thus opportunity for survey reports offering clear comparisons and analyses. Something that has been relatively little documented in previous decades is the accumulating experience of regulation itself. As regulatory bodies change their remit and their practices to take account of deregulation, it is important to find out whether the regulators, in widely different systems and societies, feel that they are succeeding in meeting the objectives set them.

Does Italian officialdom, for example, regard its attempt to recover from the disaster of the sudden 1977 deregulation as having been effective? Is the British attempt to put a stop to the (allegedly) excessively interfering practices of its previous regulatory body, the Independent Broadcasting Authority (and substitute contractual controls after a franchise auction) going to satisfy those who instigated the change? Will Americans continue to want a Fairness Doctrine—as Congress but not the FCC does—and a prohibition on cross-ownership in the same market in the era of the greatest media abundance? Will Canadians continue to feel beleaguered by the American media, even when that same abundance offers them the chance to have a wide variety of their own Canadian-based materials?

Those are a few of the vast body of newly emerging questions. These may, many of them, appear to be matters of administration or of politics. But they are all also issues of culture. And as such, one cannot hope to find any eternally valid answers to them—merely better ways to ask them.

★　★　★　★　★　★　★

Background Reading

★　★　★　★　★　★　★

This is by no means an exhaustive list of currently available materials on the subject of globalization of the media industries. It is little more than a small personal selection of books and papers that I found of particular interest and help.

Beniger, J. R., *The Control Revolution: Technological and Economic Origins of the Information Society*, Harvard University Press, 1986.

de Bens, E., and Knoche, M., *Electronic Mass Media in Europe: Prospects and Developments*, D. Reidel Publishing Company, 1987.

Dyson, K., Humphreys, P., Negrine, R., and Simon, J., *Broadcasting and the New Media Politics in Western Europe*, Routledge, 1988.

Dyson, K., and Humphreys, P., *The Politics of the Communications Revolution in Western Europe*, Frank Cass, 1987.

Eger, John M., "Global Television: An Executive Overview," *Columbia Journal of World Business* 22, no. 3, Fall 1987.

Fairburn, J., and Kay, J., eds., *Mergers and Merger Policy*, Oxford University Press, 1989.

Ferguson, M., ed., *New Communications Technologies and the Public Interest,* Sage Publications, 1986.

Gannett Center Journal of Columbia University, *The New Media Barons,* Winter 1989, special edition.

Levitt, Theodore, "The Globalization of Markets," *Harvard Business Review,* May/June 1983.

McQuail, D., and Davin, S., eds., "New Media Politics: Comparative Perspectives in Western Europe," Euromedia Research Group, 1986.

Media, Culture & Society, *West European Broadcasting* 2, no. 1, January 1989 (special edition).

Obuchowski, Janice, "Comprehensive Study of the Globalization of Mass Media Firms," National Telecommunications and Information Administration, U.S. Department of Commerce, February 1990.

OECD, "Fusions Internationales et la Politique de Concurrence," OECD Publications, Paris, 1990

Television Business International, *The New Order in Europe,* November/December 1988 (special edition).

Index

Acquisitions and mergers, 1, 10, 23, 24-26, 27-28, 53, 61-62; benefits of, 8-9, 50; regulation of, 51, 56, 57, 62, 65
Agnelli, Gianni, 32
Asia, 36
Audience, 7, 11, 15, 50; television, 4, 5, 19, 27, 31, 34, 66, 67. *See also* Minority audiences; Readership
Australia, 2, 23, 28, 50

BBC (British Broadcasting Corporation), 4, 19, 47, 48
Berlusconi, Silvio, 21, 30-34, 66
Bertelsmann Inc., 22, 24, 26, 37-39
Broadcasting, 15-16, 25-26, 69-70; regulation of, 13, 41, 49-50, 54-58. *See also* Public broadcasting; Radio; Television
Broadcasting Standards Council (Great Britain), 53

Cable television, 4, 31, 55, 60, 62, 65
Censorship, 53
Channel Four (Great Britain), 3, 4, 47
Communications Act (United States), 48-49, 54-55, 62-63
Competition, 4, 14, 17, 27, 39, 41, 42, 43; government role in, 3, 13, 32, 38, 49-51, 54-58, 59-61, 65-68. *See also* Industrial concentration

Costs, 2-3, 4, 9, 10, 23, 28, 60
Cross-ownership, 1, 13, 24-25, 27, 38, 46, 50, 53-55, 65, 66, 75
Cultural environment, 12, 22, 23, 39, 42, 66, 67, 72, 76
Cultural policy, 5-6

Denationalization, 46-47
Deregulation, 3, 4, 5, 7, 39, 46, 48-50, 55-57, 66; goal of, 9. *See also* Privatization; Regulation

Eastern Europe, 32, 45
Economies of scale, 9, 10, 30, 58
Eisner, Michael, 28
Electromagnetic spectrum, 16, 48, 56, 57, 69, 71, 72
Entertainment industry, 2, 35-36. *See also* Broadcasting; Film industry
Europe, 51, 61
European Community, 6-7

FCC (Federal Communications Commission), 49, 54-57, 59, 60, 62, 71
Film industry, 22-24, 28-29, 31, 36, 56, 61
Fininvest Group, 31, 33-34
Finland, 43, 47, 64
Foreign ownership, 23-24, 31, 32, 33, 46, 58-59, 61, 66; regulation of, 2, 52, 62-63

Foreign sales, 6, 22, 29-30, 34
France, 3, 33, 42, 45, 46, 64
Franchises, 13, 23, 65
Freedom of information, 6, 12-13,
    20, 51, 53, 54, 55, 73-75, 76
Freedom of the press, 11, 12, 75
Frequency spectrum. See Elec-
    tromagnetic spectrum

Germany, 31, 38, 39, 48, 64
Globalization of the media, 1, 10.
    See also Industrial concentra-
    tion; Ownership of the media
Global localizing, 35
Government and the media, 12, 31,
    46, 66-67, 73. See also Competi-
    tion, government role in; Regula-
    tion
Great Britain, 18-19, 45-46, 47,
    52-53, 61, 72; regulation in, 33,
    53, 57, 64-66; television in, 3-4,
    23, 48

Hersant, Robert, 33
Homogenization of media, 3, 25

Independence of the media, 3, 18,
    25, 50-51, 52-53, 60, 73-74
Independent Television Commission
    (Great Britain), 64-65
Industrial concentration, 11-12, 13,
    18, 23, 58-59, 64, 71, 73, 75; na-
    tional, 1, 30-31, 49, 50, 70. See
    also Acquisitions and mergers
Influence of media, 18-20, 70-71
Information revolution, 8-10, 12-13
Information services, 3, 16, 20, 44,
    48, 70, 71-72
Ireland, 5, 66
Italy, 23, 34, 42, 48; regulation in,
    20-32, 64, 66

Japan, 14, 24
Journalism, 11, 53. See also
    Newspaper publishing

Kennedy, Edward, 53, 54
Kirch, Leo, 39
Kraemer, Juergen, 26

Legislation, 31-32, 33, 50-51, 53-54,
    55-56, 57, 62, 64-65. See also
    specific legislation, e.g., Commu-
    nications Act (United States)
Liberalization of the media, 47-48
Licenses, 19, 35, 47, 52, 62-63, 64
Lippmann, Walter, 14
Local ownership, 13, 49, 52, 60, 66
Local regulation, 38, 67
London Observer (newspaper), 42,
    44-45

Management of the media, 2, 28,
    34-35, 36-37, 59
Marketing, 4-5, 60, 62
Markets, 22, 23, 29-30
Maxwell, Robert, 2, 42, 46
Media: economics of, 10, 13, 14-15,
    23, 27-28, 34, 38-39, 47, 48, 70-71;
    role of, 17-18, 43. See also Costs;
    Competition; Ownership of the
    media
Mergers. See Acquisitions and
    mergers
Minority audiences, 5, 49
Mohn, Reinhard, 37
Monopolies and Mergers Commis-
    sion (Great Britain), 57, 65
Monopoly. See Industrial concen-
    tration
MTV Network, 26, 47
Multiple ownership, 13, 49, 52,
    54-56
Murdoch, Rupert, 2, 21, 29, 50, 52,
    53-54, 55, 57. See also News Cor-
    poration Ltd.
Murdock, Graham, 46-49

Nationalism, 2. See also Trans-
    nationalism

News Corporation Ltd., 19, 23, 24, 26-28, 30, 41, 61

Newspaper Conservation Act (United States), 56

Newspaper ownership, 1, 2, 42-43, 50, 57, 59, 65-66

Newspaper publishing, 11, 13-14, 39, 44-45, 52-53, 56, 70, 75

Office of Fair Trading (Great Britain), 65

Ownership of the media, 2, 15, 17, 33, 41-42, 43-44, 70; regulation of, 13, 51-52, 54-58, 62-63. *See also* Acquisitions and mergers; specific types of ownership, e.g., Cross-ownership; Newspaper ownership

Politics and the media, 5, 13-14, 32-33, 39, 42, 51, 52-53, 59, 63

Power of the media, 13, 44, 59, 60, 70

Press Complaints Commission (Great Britain), 53

Prime Time Access Rule (United States), 59-60

Privatization, 45-50

Production companies, 3-4, 23, 31, 56, 60, 62

Public broadcasting, 49, 56; commercialization of, 47, 48

Public interest, 71, 76

Publishing industry, 2, 15, 24, 27, 31, 34, 38. *See also* Newspaper publishing

Radio, 47, 52, 54-55, 64, 65, 66

Readership, 14, 18-19

Regulation, 2, 12, 13, 14, 16-17, 30, 38, 41, 76; goal of, 51. *See also* Deregulation; Legislation

Reregulation, 47, 49, 50

Rowland, Roland ("Tiny"), 44-45

Satellite systems, 19, 29, 30, 31, 38, 55, 60, 66-67

Scandinavia, 42, 43, 47

Social implications, 2, 17-20, 51, 53, 76. *See also* Cultural environment

Sony Corporation, 21-22, 24, 34-37, 41, 61

Spain, 33

Sports channels, 32, 39

Subsidies, 14, 43, 63, 66-67

Takeovers. *See* Acquisitions and mergers

Technology and the media, 2-3, 7-9, 10, 13, 15-16, 22, 35, 36, 61

Telecommunication, 7, 15-16, 55, 57, 71-72

Television, 4-5, 30-31, 34, 47, 49, 56, 59-61, 70. *See also* Audience, television; Cable television; MTV Network; Sports channels

Television ownership, 3, 32, 33, 38-39, 42, 46, 52, 62

Television programs, 36, 59-60, 61

"Television Without Frontiers" (green paper), 6

Time Warner Inc., 21, 24-26

Transnationalism, 5-7, 15

Turner, Ted, 44, 50

United Kingdom. *See* Great Britain

United States, 4, 36, 42, 44, 61; regulation in, 13, 46, 48-50, 51-52, 53-58, 71; and Western Europe, 6, 23, 29-30

Vertical integration, 26, 36, 41, 56, 60, 62

Walt Disney Company, 21, 28-30

Western Europe, 4, 5-7, 14, 42-43, 63-67

Wössner, Mark, 37